外宣微记

理论与实践
THEORY AND PRACTICE

译路行远

刘强 著

跨越差异的国际传播

序

《译路行远：跨越差异的国际传播》终于与读者见面了，可喜可贺。该书是"外宣微记"主笔刘强又一部有关国际传播与翻译的著作。相较之前出版的《笔尖上的文化碰撞：对外话语与翻译》，该书更为系统地阐发了对跨越语言差异、文化差异、叙事方式差异"三道难关"，走好国际传播"最后一公里"的思考。

每一种语言都有其独特的文化基因，在翻译转换过程中，很难做到斤两相称，严丝合缝。该书也提醒读者，每一种语言必然伴生着与之适应的叙事方式，忽视叙事方式的差异而进行简单的翻译，很可能会影响国际传播效果。翻译有其自身的标准和原则，传播也有自身的逻辑和规律，二者难免会有冲突。2021年，英国汉学家蓝诗玲（Julia Lovell）"翻译+改写（translation+reworking）"了《西游记》，而非纯粹地去"翻译"，目的是让中国古典名著在英文世界传播得更远。举例来说，原著中诸如"婴儿姹女（Baby and Fair Girl）""三花聚顶（three flowers joined on top）""五气朝元（five breaths faced their source）"等道家术语和法门，中国人尚且不能完全明白，更何况外国读者。我们如果讲"效果导向"，就不能"一译了之"，要有"reworking"的意识和能力，这也是构建融通中外的话语体系的关键所在。

《译路行远：跨越差异的国际传播》的一个独到之处在于，作者结合国际传播与时政话语英译实践，从新闻编辑部视角，总结归纳了国际主流英文媒体的话语特点，并进一步分析了中国时政话语的特点及其英译难点。该书通过鲜活翔实的案例，展示了语言中的叙事与文化差异，在话语对比中思考跨越差异之道。英国汉学家祁立天（Tim Clissold）说："中文的不精确，会让世界各地的会计和理赔员火冒三丈，然而……正是这份不精确给读者提供了空间。"（《云室：一个英国人眼中的中国古诗》）在《倚天屠龙记》里，张无忌答应替赵敏做三件事，前提是"不违侠义之道"。这抽象又模糊的"侠义"二字给张无忌留下了足够的"阐释空间"。中文的抽象与模糊恰恰是对外表达的一大难题，尤其当"义利""道""天""仁"等中国传统文化概念进入当下的时政话语，时刻考验着国际传播工作者的语言和文化素养。

《中庸》有云："君子之道，辟如行远必自迩，辟如登高必自卑。"塑造可信可爱可敬的中国形象，是一项长期工程。国际传播工作者要有"行远必自迩，登高必自卑"的务实精神，不急不躁，不好高骛远。

该书是作者在国际传播与翻译道路上"远行"的阶段性总结与心得体会，延续了作者力求"有趣、有料、有态度"的写作风格，对于学习外语和从事翻译及对外传播工作的读者来说，是一部有益的参考书籍。作为作者的同事，我为他感到高兴，也希望他在今后的国际传播与翻译道路上继续深耕，行稳致远，进而有为。

中国互联网新闻中心党委书记、总编辑

中国翻译协会副会长　　王晓辉

北京语言大学博士生导师

前言

印度裔英国作家萨尔曼·拉什迪（Salman Rushdie）在其名篇"Is Nothing Sacred?"一文中对比小说与宗教的区别：

> Whereas religion seeks to privilege one language above all others, one set of values above all others, one text above all others, the novel has always been about the way in which different languages, values and narratives quarrel, and about the shifting relations between them.
>
> 宗教试图尊奉一种语言于其他语言之上，尊奉一套价值观于其他价值观之上，尊奉一部文本于其他文本之上，而小说常常是关于不同语言、价值观和叙事之间的争论，以及三者之间不断变换的关系。

这段话有三个关键词："languages（语言）""values（价值观）""narratives（叙事）"。在拉什迪看来，小说更包容，允许不同语言、价值观、叙事之间共存、互动、争论。

拉什迪的"小说观"对国际传播工作很有启发。国际传播，本质上就是"语言""价值观""叙事"这三者之间的共存、互动乃至争论。笔者仿效拉什迪的话描述国际传播工作的特点：International communication has always been about the way in which different languages, values and narratives quarrel, but do so in peace.（国际传播常常是关于不同语言、价值观和叙事之间的争论，但方式却是和谐的。）

国际传播要跨越"三道关":语言差异、文化(价值观)差异、叙事(方式)差异。近些年,国际传播逐渐成为热门话题,"讲好中国故事""融通中外"成了时髦语。但漂亮话好说,漂亮事难做。不懂语言的细节,不懂中英文叙事有别,不懂文化和价值观的差异,空有对国际传播工作"指点江山"的豪情与热情,终究是无益的空谈。要融通中外,就必须首先正视这三种差异。正视差异不是为了分优劣、定权威,而是在尊重差异的基础上,超越差异、求同存异,用和平理性的方式应对因差异引起的误解乃至分歧。

跨越"三道关"首先离不开翻译工作,翻译是国际传播工作的基础工程。但我们还应认识到翻译在国际传播工作中的局限性,因为翻译有翻译的标准和原则,传播有传播的逻辑和规律。翻译与国际传播绝不可画等号。

曾英译《鲁迅小说全集》的英国作家、汉学家蓝诗玲(Julia Lovell)说:"他(鲁迅)令我经常停下思考的写作习惯是,经常、故意地重复。……将此重复准确地译出,在英语读者看来,既不舒服,又不高雅,所以有时候我会对此做一些变换。"(吕奇,《汉学家蓝诗玲译者风格多维研究》)蓝诗玲这段话讲了一个道理:把中文不加任何"变换"而"准确地译出",不一定被英文读者喜欢,不一定取得预期的传播效果。

为什么需要"变换"?因为中英文叙事方式大有不同。英文"narrative"既可以表示"叙事(a story)",比如"a narrative of China threat(中国威胁论)",又可以表示"叙事方式(the art, technique, or process of narrating)"(《美国传统词典》)。哈佛大学教授安东尼·赛奇(Anthony Saich)在一次访谈中提醒中英叙事有别:"中文的叙事方式在中国受欢迎,但在说英语的地方就不那么受欢迎了。"

语言与叙事方式,好比"皮"与"毛"。每一种语言必然伴生着与之适应的叙事方式。叙事方式有差异而无优劣。常记叙事差异,就要时刻警惕"把翻译等同于国际传播"的错误认知与做法。

很多情况下，按照翻译标准生产出来的内容并不能满足国际传播的叙事要求。外行常常天真地把会外语等同于会翻译，把翻译等同于国际传播，这种严重低估翻译与国际传播专业性和复杂性的认知常常令人沮丧。

除了语言和叙事差异，直面中外两个舆论场的国际传播工作者还时刻感受着文化（价值观）差异带来的冲击。所谓文化差异，说白了就是一种文化里能接受甚至引以为傲的事情，受另一种文化熏陶的人不一定能接受，甚至会强力排斥。

人们往往习惯以固有的认知方式去审视异样的文化，这是思维惯性，也构成文化阻力。梁漱溟先生在《东西文化及其哲学》一书中指出："（中国人）对西方人之要求自由，总怀两种态度：一种是淡漠底很，不懂要这个作什么；一种是吃惊底很，以为这岂不乱天下！"在如今喧嚣复杂的中外舆论场，无论是以中国思维看世界，还是以西方思维看中国，都会陷入"看不懂、看不透"的危险处境，结果是在各自心里产生一个想象的对方罢了。

笔者在《笔尖上的文化碰撞：对外话语与翻译》一书中提出，国际传播工作者要"对外表达"与"对内科普"两条腿走路。本书依然坚持这一初心使命，从"语言""叙事""文化"三个维度分享国际传播工作实践中的心得体会，思考对外表达的困境与突破之道。

本书第一章聚焦国际主流英文媒体的话语风格，从句法、用词、节奏、细节、修辞、标题等六个方面介绍国际主流英文媒体的写作特点。读外媒，既读语言，也读观点、读文化，这是"知己知彼"、对外讲好中国故事的关键一步，也是构建融通中外的话语体系的必然要求。

第二章总结了中国时政话语的五个特点，并从"外媒视角""汉学家视角"观中国时政话语英译的落地情况。本章结合具体案例，总结在英译隐喻、夸张、用典等修辞手法时常陷入的误区，探讨中英叙事冲突影响下翻译在国际传播中的局限性。

第三章聚焦中西"政府观"差异视域下的国际传播身份困境

与突破之道。本章希望回答三个问题:"政府观"差异如何影响中国叙事的流量与公信力;中国叙事面临怎样的外部舆论环境;如何突破讲好中国故事的"身份困境"。

第四章浅谈以 ChatGPT 为代表的生成式人工智能技术对翻译、新闻写作、社交媒体运营带来的机遇与挑战。2022 年 11 月 30 日,美国人工智能公司 OpenAI 面向公众开放 ChatGPT。2023 年 3 月 14 日,微软官方网站发布声明,确认新版必应搜索引擎(New Bing)已嵌入 GPT-4,实现了 Bing 与 ChatGPT 的深度融合(本书统一称之为 Bing GPT)。2023 年 3 月 21 日,谷歌推出与 ChatGPT、Bing GPT 抗衡的生成式人工智能产品 Google Bard(现已更名为 Gemini)。国内众多高科技企业也竞相投入研发,掀起"百模大战"。未来,生成式人工智能势必对翻译与国际传播产生深刻影响。译者、记者、编辑等文字工作者该如何应对?是轻言"取代",还是主动拥抱技术?如何让人工智能成为辅助我们工作的利器?

对外讲好中国故事,构建融通中外的话语体系,说来容易做来难。没有扎实的双语功底,不懂语言、叙事与文化差异,单凭一腔热情和"左突右撞"的蛮力,很难塑造可信、可爱、可敬的中国形象。未来,国际传播的主体一定是懂语言、懂叙事、懂文化的中国人。当前,国际传播人才培养依然任重道远。本书延续笔者一贯的视角与风格——细读外媒、戏说翻译、戏说中外,既有微观的话语分析和比较,也有宏观的文化思考,展示翻译与国际传播的乐趣与挑战。希望本书能启迪更多年轻读者参与翻译与国际传播事业。

本书内容源于工作实践,囿于笔者的学识、见识,难免存在不妥之处,恳请方家批评指正。

刘 强
2024 年 3 月 1 日

目录

第一章 外媒话语探微：媒体视角 / 001

1.1 句法 / 005

    1.1.1 右分支句 / 005

    1.1.2 长短相宜：悦目悦耳 / 009

1.2 用词 / 013

1.3 节奏 / 023

    1.3.1 凑韵 / 023

    1.3.2 "凑三"规则 / 028

1.4 细节 / 032

    1.4.1 受众意识 / 032

    1.4.2 营造画面 / 036

    1.4.3 有的放矢 / 039

1.5 修辞 / 043

    1.5.1 隐喻 / 043

    1.5.2 用典 / 047

    1.5.3 转喻等其他修辞 / 051

1.6 标题 / 055

第二章 中国时政话语：译路维艰 / 063

2.1 时政话语英译 / 065

    2.1.1 时政话语特点分析 / 068

  2.1.2 外媒视角 / 106

  2.1.3 汉学家视角 / 111

 2.2 翻译中的误解与误用 / 116

  2.2.1 隐喻的误解 / 119

  2.2.2 夸张的误用 / 130

  2.2.3 用典的问题 / 137

第三章　国际传播：困境与突破 / 147

 3.1 文化差异 / 149

 3.2 身份困境 / 152

 3.3 突破之道 / 156

  3.3.1 谁来讲 / 157

  3.3.2 "话语权"再思考 / 159

第四章　ChatGPT：机遇与挑战 / 165

 4.1 ChatGPT 与时政话语英译 / 167

  4.1.1 句法 / 168

  4.1.2 词汇 / 172

  4.1.3 修辞手法 / 176

 4.2 ChatGPT 赋能翻译学习 / 181

  4.2.1 识别用典、夸张等修辞手法 / 184

  4.2.2 识别谐音梗 / 186

  4.2.3 破解语言"疑难杂症" / 187

  4.2.4 根据风格要求润色文字 / 189

 4.3 ChatGPT 与公示语翻译 / 191

 4.4 活用 ChatGPT 辨析同义词 / 197

第一章 外媒话语探微：媒体视角

常有读者在笔者的个人微信公众号"外宣微记"留言询问：为什么阅读国内英文媒体时感觉游刃有余，阅读英美报刊等外媒却总感卡顿吃力？如何改进学习方法才能更流畅地读懂外媒？

国内不少英文学习者通过阅读英文报刊积累英文表达，这的确是提升英文水平的一种法门。但是，学习者首先要认识到，阅读英文媒体的文字，无论是即时新闻，还是新闻特写，抑或是时事评论，都是在阅读新闻体英语。既然是新闻英语，就必然有新闻专业门槛。

同样是阅读英文媒体，尤其是阅读英美报刊，以积累单词短语为目的的英文学习者所关注的角度必然与受过新闻写作专业训练的记者编辑不同。从编辑部视角审视一篇外媒文章，有很多"细节"或者说"评判标准"值得关注：标题（headline）、导语（lead）、正文结构（structure）、句法（syntax）、事件背景（context）、细节描摹（details）、选词用词逻辑（word choices）、节奏感（rhythm）的把握、修辞手法（figures of speech）的运用。

阅读外媒感到吃力，未必是词汇量不足，也许是不谙外媒写作"套路"所致。若能学会从编辑部视角品读外媒，懂得如何品评文字优劣，既能开卷有益，又能开卷有趣（pleasant and profitable reading）。

从目前的全球话语格局来看，国际主流英文媒体依然手握"金话筒"，占据舆论高地。有鉴于此，用英文讲好中国故事依然是国际传播工作的重中之重。所谓"知己知彼，百战不殆"，读懂外媒的行文逻辑和叙事特点，是我们改进国际传播方式方法的关键一步，也是构建融通中外的话语体系的题中之意。中国故事若要说得出、传得开、叫得响，国际传播工作者就不能不主动学习外媒话语特点，取长补短。

美国资深媒体人、《俄勒冈人报》(*The Oregonian*) 前总编杰克·哈特 (Jack Hart) 曾归纳优质写作 (good writing) 普遍具备的七个特点：

1. 行文有力，富有感染力 (radiates energy)；
2. 主题明确，不拐弯抹角 (gets to the point)；
3. 用字形象，画面感强 (rich in color)；
4. 语气适宜 (has a tone appropriate to the subject)；
5. 文字富有节奏 (has a rhythm)；
6. 表达清楚易懂 (clear)；
7. 语法体例严谨规范 (mechanically correct)。

(*Wordcraft: The Complete Guide to Clear, Powerful Writing*,《选词的艺术：如何让写作清晰有力》)

以上七条不妨作为我们以编辑部视角品评外媒写作优劣的总纲，也是指导我们进一步改进英文写作风格可参照的标准。

《尚书》说："学，效也。"笔者结合品读外媒以及英文新闻写作与改稿实践经验，从句法、用词、节奏、细节、修辞、标题等六个方面详细展开，从外媒中撷取优质案例，供读者参考。

Easy reading is damn hard writing.

– Nathaniel Hawthorne

1.1 句法

1.1.1 右分支句

英国作家昆廷·克里斯普（Quentin Crisp）提醒写作者要特别注意句法清晰：

Muddled syntax is the outward and audible sign of confused minds.

句法混乱清楚地暴露了思维混乱。

美国作家、资深写作指导罗伊·彼得·克拉克（Roy Peter Clark）指出，现代美国英语最重要的句法结构就是"右分支句（right-branching sentence）"（*Wordcraft*，《选词的艺术》）。维基百科这样定义"右分支句"：

In English grammar, *a right-branching sentence* is a sentence in which the main subject of the sentence is described first, and is followed by a sequence of modifiers that provide additional information about the subject.

一个句子的主语、谓语好比一棵树的主干，主干应尽早显现，其他补充成分好比树枝，依次向外伸展。

在新闻英语中，"右分支"结构之所以受到青睐，是因为这样的结构将重要信息前置，读起来一目了然，减少阅读阻力。请看《华盛顿邮报》报道印度列车脱轨相撞事故开篇第一段：

At least 233 people were killed and more than 900 injured in eastern India on Friday after a train derailment spilled onto the opposite track and another train collided with the overturned coaches, officials told local media outlets. (*The Washington Post*, June 2, 2023)

如果把"after"引导的从句前置，虽无语法问题，但导致信息主次颠倒，加重读者阅读负担。试比较：

After a train derailment spilled onto the opposite track and another train collided with the overturned coaches, at least 233 people were killed and more than 900 injured in eastern India on Friday, officials told local media outlets.

英文新闻报道惯用"倒金字塔"结构，即，重要的信息前置，越往后，内容重要性越低。因此，在新闻写作中，开篇几段作为文章的"起手式"，表达务必清晰流畅，才能吸引读者"顺藤摸瓜"读下去。BBC报道美国犹他州（初）中小学把《圣经》列为禁书，开篇两段均采用"右分支"结构：

A school district in the US state of Utah has removed the Bible from elementary and middle schools for containing "vulgarity and violence".

The move follows a complaint from a parent that the King James Bible has material unsuitable for children. (BBC, June 3, 2023)

第一句"A school district ... removed the Bible ... for ...",第二句"The move follows a complaint that...",结构清晰,句意明了,衔接流畅,不拖泥带水。

相反,若"起手式"便给读者"云山雾罩"的感觉,多半会令人生厌。杰克·哈特在《选词的艺术》(*Wordcraft*)一书中列举了《纽约时报》一则反面案例:

After a long campaign of ideological clashes, policy debates, and talk of a grand reckoning on the direction of the Democratic Party, the presidential primaries starting on Monday will be shaped by a less lofty but increasingly urgent matter: determining the best incumbent who has already proved to be a political survivor.

这段话的信息"主干"是"the presidential primaries ... will be shaped by a ... matter",但是,在"主干"浮出水面之前,长达22个单词、内含多个介词短语的句子(After...)几乎把读者绕晕了,读者须"跋山涉水"方见"庐山真面"。按照"右分支"结构修改如下:

The Democratic primary campaign now boils down to a key question. For months the campaign swirled around lofty issues of ideology, policy, and party philosophy. But on Monday Iowa chooses, and from here on the outcome hinges on who voters think can beat Donald Trump.

修改后的版本调整为三句话，每句话都是"右分支"结构，比原来错综复杂的长句读起来清爽许多。尤其第一句以"boils down to a question"结尾，设置悬念，很自然地引导读者读下去。

笔者读外媒也曾遇到不少"云山雾罩"的句子，比如《纽约时报》这句：

[Anti-Trump texts by the lead F.B.I. investigator, a former F.B.I. director who put Mr. Trump in a bad light through improper disclosure of F.B.I. documents and information, transgressions by F.B.I. and Justice Department officials in securing permission to surveil a Trump associate and more] were condemned by the Justice Department's inspector general even as he found no direct evidence of political bias in the investigation. (*The New York Times*, August 8, 2023)

读完此句，笔者第一感受就是"有点绕（a bit convoluted）"。"主语（subject）"部分拉得太长，且主语四个成分结构很不协调：

1. anti-Trump texts by the lead F.B.I. investigator；

2. a former F.B.I. director who put Mr. Trump in a bad light through improper disclosure of F.B.I. documents and information；

3. transgressions by F.B.I. and Justice Department officials in securing permission to surveil a Trump associate;

4. and more.

经历主语的千回百折之后，读者终于见到了句子的谓语部分"were condemned by"。这样的复杂句加重了读者的阅读负担。可以按照"右分支"结构修改，把被动句改为主动句，宾语部分结构尽量匀称些，整句话也不妨断为两句。比如：

The Justice Department's inspector general <u>condemned the anti-Trump texts</u> of the lead F.B.I. investigator, <u>the improper disclosure</u> of F.B.I. documents and information by a former F.B.I. director, and <u>the F.B.I.'s use</u> of a secret warrant to surveil a Trump associate without proper justification. However, he found no direct evidence of political bias in the investigation.

读外媒，先读"起手式"；读"起手式"，先观句法结构。清晰有力的句法结构，一定能吸引读者停留驻足。但凡要闻大事，主流英文媒体都会报道，我们不妨养成对比阅读的习惯，品评优劣，取长补短，学以致用。

1.1.2 长短相宜：悦目悦耳

英国作家毛姆特别赞赏美国作家霍桑（小说《红字》的作者）驾驭句子的能力，称赞霍桑能写出长达半页但结构匀称、句意清晰、引人共鸣的句子。在《书与你》（*Books and You*）一书中，毛姆写道：

Authors then will be glad to learn from Hawthorne how to manage a sentence of more than half a dozen words, how to combine dignity with lucidity, and how without pedantry to <u>please both the eye and the ear</u>.

霍桑不但能驾驭长句，还能兼顾文字的品格与清澈，让文字悦目又悦耳，这应该是所有文字工作者追求的目标。曾有读者留言提问：在翻译或者写作中，多写长句好，还是多写短句好？

这个问题的答案只能是：It depends.（看情况）。

短句与长句，各有优势，各有用武之地。写作者应根据语境需要善加"调配"，该长则长，该短则短，尤其要注重长短搭配。善于变换句子长短，是让文字悦耳悦目（please both the eye and the ear）的一项重要技巧。请看《经济学人》如何用"短句重复"给文字增加节奏感：

The capital's centre escaped the worst of the flooding, but suburbs and towns to its south and west suffered. <u>Over 1.6m people were evacuated. Tens of thousands of homes were destroyed. Bridges and roads were damaged.</u> (*The Economist*, August 10, 2023)

重复短小精悍的句子，也是欧美政要常用的演讲技巧。请看美国前总统奥巴马 2012 年胜选演讲词：

That's the future we hope for. That's the vision we share. That's where we need to go.

除了短句重复，长短句相互烘托也是让文字悦耳的重要技巧。

请看《经济学人》如何在长句后接短句：

> Still, it is possible that Mr Erdogan may start to listen not just to his opponents, but also to impartial experts and technocrats who were once close to him, especially over his ruinous economic policies. <u>He certainly should.</u> (*The Economist*, May 31, 2023)

结尾只有三个单词的短句 "He certainly should." 铿锵有力，好似一声锣鼓，余音回味。

还可以短句引出长句。请看米歇尔·奥巴马 2020 年演讲词：

> <u>The job is hard.</u> It requires clear-headed judgment, a mastery of complex and competing issues, a devotion to facts and history, a moral compass, and an ability to listen – and an abiding belief that each of the 330,000,000 lives in this country has meaning and worth.

"The job is hard." 既直抒胸臆又唤起读者注意，请读者静听（当总统）这项工作为何不容易，为紧随其后包含 40 多个单词的长句（It requires...）做好铺垫。试想，若把这两句揉成一句（The hard job requires...），长短句相互烘托的层次感和节奏感便荡然无存。讲话者说得累，听者也听着烦。

《经济学人》报道塔利班 2023 年在阿富汗全境开展铲除罂粟种植运动，并介绍塔利班上一次执政期间也曾禁止种植罂粟。《经济学人》先以短句 "The Taliban have form." 起头（have form: have a history or a record of doing something），然后以长句展开，详细介绍塔利班当年的"禁毒"史。

> **The Taliban have form.** They banned poppy cultivation during their previous spell in power, in 2000, with similar results. It duly dropped from around 82,000 hectares in 2000 to less than 8,000 in 2001. The ban was rolled back only later that year, amid the looming prospect of an invasion by America and its allies. (*The Economist*, June 22, 2023)

读外媒,不但要会看,还要会听。遇到富有节奏的句子,不妨轻声读出来,细细品味。工作实践中,无论是编辑文章还是润色译文,既要用眼,也要用耳。

翻译党的二十大报告期间,笔者曾与几位同事在审校环节朗读译文,目的是在"听审"中给译文再把脉、再校准。有时,目之所及并不觉译文别扭,读出来一听却是另一个感觉。"诗圣"杜甫改诗也用耳,"新诗改罢自长吟"。天才如杜甫,推敲诗作也要"长吟",而不是闷声琢磨。好的文字一定是赏心悦目又悦耳。中英文在这一点上是相通的。

The most valuable of all talents is that of never using two words when one will do.

– Thomas Jefferson

1.2 用词

朱熹说："辞，取达意而止，不以富丽为工。"《圣经》有云："How forcible are right words!"（Job 6:25）

新闻写作要言之有物、言之有力。这就要求选词用词切忌含含糊糊。比如，如果把报道对象模糊写作"the man/woman"并不合格，这说明记者的采访工作未做到位。采访对象是"student"还是"taxi driver"，应尽量具体化。《金融时报》报道电影《芭比》在中国备受女性观众喜欢，开篇第一句这样写：

Beijing law student Feifei enjoyed the *Barbie* movie so much she went to see it twice this week, each time wearing a bright-pink baseball cap. (*Financial Times*, July 29, 2023)

"Beijing law student"比笼统地写"Beijing girl"更具体化，交代的信息也更多。

笔者在工作中改到这样一段文字：

The international sporting event, which has captivated global attention, was hailed by Chen Weiya, the chief director of the opening ceremony, as an opportunity for young <u>individuals</u> from diverse backgrounds to foster friendship on an international stage.

从新闻写作的视角，"individuals"过于笼统，也有些生硬。在本段"sporting"语境下，把"individuals"改为"athletes""competitors"或者"participants"更具体，也更契合语境。

2016年，笔者在美国北卡罗来纳大学教堂山分校新闻学院访学时曾做过这样一项课堂作业：用一段英文描写某人酒后驾车逃避警车追赶，要求不用或尽量少用形容词和副词，但文字要有画面感，要写得有声有色。

这项任务的挑战在于，既然要把修饰词出现的频率降至最低，那就只能在动词和名词上下功夫，要选择"自带画面感"的动词或名词，才能实现文字"有声有色"的效果。路透社前资深记者安娜·麦凯恩（Anna Mckane）把这样的词称为"listen-to-me words"或者"attention-grabbing words"。（*News Writing*,《新闻写作》）

美国作家、资深编辑威廉姆·津瑟（William Zinsser）特别强调动词在新闻写作中的地位：动词是写作中最重要的工具，因为是动词推着句子前进，是动词给句子赋能。……很多动词，如"glitter""dazzle""poke""scatter""pamper""beguile""swagger""twirl""vex"等，它们本身的意象（imagery）或发音（sound）中就透着词义。也许没有哪种语言像英语这样拥有大量色彩鲜明的动词。……表达要精准，动词选择要精准。（*On Writing Well*,《写作法宝：非虚构写作指南》）

动词越具体（specific），指向就越精准，读者就越能如亲临新闻现场一般感知事件原貌。比如，描写某人酒后驾车狂飙，动词"barrel down the street"就比"speed down the street"有画面感，因为"speed"比较抽象，画面略朦胧，"barrel"相比而言则更具体，兼具"move rapidly"与"move recklessly"双重内涵。

barrel: to move very fast in a particular direction, <u>especially in a way that you cannot control</u> (*Oxford Advanced American Dictionary*)

2023年两会期间，外交部曾以"狂飙"喻中美关系，画面感十足，受到外媒广泛关注：

"如果美方不踩刹车，<u>继续沿着错误道路狂飙下去</u>，再多的护栏也挡不住脱轨翻车，必然陷入冲突对抗。"

外交部这样翻译：

If the United States does not hit the brake but continues to <u>speed down the wrong path</u>, no amount of guardrails can prevent derailing, and there will surely be conflict and confrontation. (March 7, 2023)

在众多外媒报道中，英国《金融时报》表现与众不同，没有照搬外交部译文，尤其在翻译"狂飙"一词时选择了更有画面感的动词"barrel"。请看：

If the US doesn't hit the brakes and continues to barrel down the wrong track, no amount of guardrails can prevent the carriage from derailing and crashing, and there will surely be conflict and confrontation. (*Financial Times*, March 7, 2023)

从"编辑部视角"读外媒，不难读懂《金融时报》以"barrel"替换"speed"的选词逻辑。

正如津瑟所言，英文中很多动词本身的意象或发音中就透着词义。比如，"whisper"从发音上就给人"speak softly and quietly"之感，这也就决定了"whisper"比动词"speak"更具体、更有画面感。同理，我们从"giggle"一词的发音中仿佛能听到"咯咯笑声"。

动词本身的意象或发音赋予词语独特的"气质"，笔者将这种气质称之为"词气（connotation）"。即便是同义词，词气也有"细微差异（nuance）"，正是这常常难以言传的"细微差异"使得同义词之间不能真正画等号。俄乌危机以来，外媒总是明里暗里地把话题引向台湾问题，且用词内含心机，国际传播者要时刻警惕。来看路透社的一段报道：

The West has been wary of China's response, with some warning that a Russian victory would color China's actions toward Taiwan. (Reuters, February 18, 2023)

英文词典告诉我们，动词"color"与"influence"同义：

to exert an influence on; affect: eg. The war colored the soldier's life. (《美国传统词典》)

从词典释义似乎看不到"color"与"influence"有何细微差异。那么，路透社编辑为何选用"color"而不直说"influence"？是单纯地追求用词多样化吗？

问题在于："color"与"influence"词气不同。如果路透社编辑选用"influence"一词，给读者的印象是：俄罗斯的胜利会直接影响台湾问题的解决，如此用词显然失之武断；用"color"一词则弱化了这层意思，给读者的印象是：俄罗斯的胜利会对台湾问题的解决产生微妙、间接的影响（subtle and indirect impact）。如此用词表面上谨慎收敛，进退自如，实则是在混淆是非。

中国时政话语英译，选词用词也要特别注意近义词之间词气的微妙差异。举笔者修改过的一个翻译案例：

完善重大疫情防控救治体系

We perfected the systems for major epidemic containment and treatment.

把"完善"译成"perfect"显然是不合适的。

perfect: to make something free from faults （《剑桥高级学习词典》）

其实不必查英文词典，我们单从字面即可感受动词"perfect"散发的那股"臻于完美"的词气。如此翻译，译文就把话说得太满了，不如使用"improve"一词更谦虚内敛。译文应尽可能贴近原文，"过"与"不及"都不合格。

久经考验的新闻编辑和译者，对词气都有较强的感知力。修炼这份感知力，无捷径可寻，需要在实践中磨炼，在阅读中感悟。

囿于应试教育下的英文学习模式，不少学习者对一些常见词的用法，认识过于片面。笔者在工作中遇到不少以"片面认知"顽固挑战"正确用法"的尴尬事例。多从"编辑部视角"思考外媒用词的逻辑，多问几个为什么，有助于拓宽词语认知，早日跳出对常见词用法的"傲慢与偏见"。举一小例。

2023年6月1日，美国总统拜登参加美国空军学院毕业典礼时不慎摔倒。美国媒体纷纷报道此事，《今日美国》用词尤其与众不同：

> President Joe Biden took a dramatic spill Thursday while passing out diplomas to graduates after giving the commencement address at the Air Force Academy in Colorado Springs, Colo. (*USA Today*, June 1, 2023)

从"编辑部视角"看，笔者不免要问几个问题：编辑为何选用"spill"一词？为何没用"fall""stumble"等更常用的词？

"spill"就是"attention-grabbing word"，成功吸引了笔者的注意。词典告诉我们，"spill"最常见的意思是"（液体）洒出、溢出"，同时还可表达"跌落"之意。请看《美国传统词典》的释义：

> n. a fall, as from a horse
>
> v. to come to the ground suddenly and involuntarily

从词典释义可以看出，"spill"可以作"fall"的同义词，但词气不同。笔者用一句英文来解释此中差异似乎更明了：

"Spill" can suggest a sense of <u>carelessness, clumsiness, or surprise</u> that might not be conveyed by the word "fall".

相比而言，"spill"比"fall"更具体、更形象，"took a dramatic spill"会让读者心生好奇：发生了什么，让总统突然摔倒？开篇能用一个词勾住读者，这样的新闻写作便成功了一半。

善用具体精准而非抽象笼统的动词、名词，不必求助形容词、副词等修饰词，是可以让文字生动起来的。表达"疫情蔓延"，经验丰富的写作者或许直接用动词"rip (across)"表达，而非"spread fast"，因为"rip"包含"to move quickly"之意。英国《卫报》曾这样评前首相鲍里斯·约翰逊执政危机："the *defenestration* of a prime minister"（*The Guardian*, January 16, 2022）。"defenestration"是一个很有画面感的词，意思是"to throw out of a window（扔出窗外）"（《美国传统词典》）。美国资深写作指导、兰登书屋执行总编本杰明·德雷尔（Benjamin Dreyer）对"defenestrate"这个词青睐有加，因为："It's just so weirdly specific."（*The New York Times*, February 1, 2019）

在新闻写作中，能以动词、名词给文章增色固然可贵，但动词、名词总免不了需要形容词、副词等修饰词的加持。把修饰词用得契合语境、不落俗套，绝非易事，要时刻谨记"辞，取达意而止，不以富丽为工"的写作宗旨。经验丰富的写作者使用修饰词往往格外小心。

杰克·哈特在《选词的艺术》一书中写道：

An accomplished writer nonetheless turns to modifiers with care.

把修饰词用得别出心裁，容易给读者留下深刻印象。英国哈里王子在新书《备胎》（Spare）中透露，初见梅根便觉得她美得"摄人心魄（heart-attack beautiful）"。用"heart-attack"修饰"beautiful"，很有创意。笔者读外媒，见到不落俗套的形容词，总会停下来细细品味学习一番。略举几例，读者可以感受一下外媒编辑部选择形容词时的用心。

  In today's sizzle-saturated media environment, White House officials understand perfectly well that an incumbent president doing his job can hardly compete for attention with a former president possibly doing time. (*The New York Times*, April 2, 2023)

用"sizzle-saturated"描述当下的媒体环境，暗含贬义。拟声词"sizzle（滋滋声）"是引申用法，喻指"轰动的、抓眼的故事（sensational and attention-grabbing stories）"。试想，在这样一个热门新闻应接不暇的媒体环境下，像前总统（特朗普）可能蹲监狱（do time）这样的轰动性新闻，当然要比现任总统（拜登）干好日常工作更能吸引人们关注。另外，"sizzle"与"saturated"构词，还有头韵修辞考虑（/s/ 音）。

  实际上，像"sizzle-saturated"这样以连字符（hyphen）构造复合词，是外媒写作常用的构词技法，体现了英文的灵活性与创造性。再看一例：

  Matt Gaetz, an ultra-Trumpy congressman from Florida, called Mr McCarthy the "biggest alligator" in the Washington swamp. (*The Economist*, January 4, 2023)

用"ultra-Trumpy"表达"extremely loyal to Trump（特朗普的死忠粉）"之意，构词凝练，幽默别致，读之令人会心一笑。

路透社报道中国超快时尚品牌Shein（希音）的运营模式，用"slick"一词修饰公司的社交媒体策略。请看：

It also has a slick social media strategy that mobilises TikTok and Instagram influencers. (Reuters, June 5, 2023)

如果单纯地夸赞，路透社完全可以用"efficient""impressive"等词，而"slick"一词既褒又贬，颇耐人寻味。笔者用一句英文阐释：

The word "slick" suggests that Shein's social media strategy is not only smooth and appealing, but also possibly deceptive or manipulative.

修饰词用得好，能起到言简义丰的效果，令读者回味。反之，修饰词若用得轻佻随意，恰恰是词汇贫乏、笔力笨拙的表现。经验丰富的写作者见到"dropped heavily""walked clumsily"，会忍不住问：为什么不用"plunge""stumble"这样简洁有力的动词呢？写作者当牢记美国著名作家斯蒂芬·金（Stephen King）的告诫：

The road to hell is paved with adverbs. (*On Writing: A Memoir of the Craft*,《写作这回事：创作生涯回忆录》)

通往地狱之路，是由副词铺就的。

读外媒，不妨把自己代入记者或编辑的角色，看到一个修饰词，不妨问一问：编辑为什么选中这个词而不用其他近义词？比如：

Pricier purchases such as new homes are, however, struggling to recover. (*The Economist*, June 1, 2023)

a punchy pledge by the G7 countries to provide Ukraine with more defence equipment (*The Economist*, July 12, 2023)

为何选用形容词"pricy"不用"expensive"？为何选用"punchy"与"pledge"搭配而不用更常用的"strong"？"pricier"比"more expensive"更省空间；"pledge"严肃正式，但"punchy"轻快活泼，二者搭配别有一番风趣。另外，"pricier purchases"与"punchy pledge"都有头韵修辞考虑（/p/ 音），读来更有节奏感。

有节奏感的文字更容易给读者留下深刻印象，对文字质量有追求的编辑部都会有意识地在这方面下点功夫。

Good things come in threes.

1.3 节奏

1.3.1 凑韵

高明的写作者善于在文字中制造节奏感。善于变换句子长短，便是制造节奏感的重要方法（1.1.2 长短相宜：悦目悦耳）。除了在句式结构上花心思，外媒编辑部在选词用词上也特别注重"凑韵"，表现形式多样，包括头韵（alliteration）、押元韵（assonance）、谐音/押辅韵（consonance）等。

带"韵"的文字节奏明快，读来轻松愉悦。音乐剧《窈窕淑女》（*My Fair Lady*）里那句"The rain in Spain stays mainly in the plain."分别在"rain""Spain""stay""mainly""plain"五个单词上重复元音 /eɪ/，节奏感强，读来朗朗上口。英文诗歌最重声韵。领略头韵与押元韵之妙，试读美国诗人爱伦·坡名作《乌鸦》（*The Raven*）中的两句：

> Once upon a midnight dreary, while I pondered, weak and weary...
> While I nodded, nearly napping, suddenly there came a tapping...

以《经济学人》为代表的英文媒体特别注重在文章中"凑韵"，往往在标题和开篇第一段就以声韵吸引读者。最常用的手法

是头韵,《经济学人》尤其擅长在新闻标题中使用头韵。略举几例,感受一下:

> Stopping Somalis from starving
>
> No lessons learned
>
> The fuel and the fire
>
> Hunger in the Horn
>
> Cutting Calories
>
> The perils of perfectionism
>
> Golf and the Gulf

《经济学人》"读者来信"专栏曾刊登一位哥本哈根读者的来信,谈的是男人的胡子,短短一段,非常幽默。编辑部给这段来信加了一个韵律感十足的小标题,请看:

> *A tash gives you panache*
>
> Certainly the moustache has been much loved in earlier times ("The great moustache comeback", July 2nd). A colleague's aunt said in the 1930s that kissing a man without a moustache was like eating an egg with no salt. (*The Economist*, July 14, 2022)

在英式英语里,"tash"是"moustache"的同义词。"panache"与"self-assurance"近义。参见《剑桥高级学习词典》释义:

> tash: (*UK informal*) for moustache
>
> panache: a stylish, original, and very confident way of doing things that makes people admire you

中文有句俗语——"嘴上无毛,办事不牢",可译为"A tash gives a man panache."。中文是反着说,且"毛"与"牢"二字押韵;英文则是正着说,且"tash"与"panache"既重复元音 /æ/,也重复辅音 /ʃ/。

《经济学人》编辑部对新闻标题中声韵的重视给笔者启发。工作中,笔者也有意识地在标题中制造节奏感。比如,一篇娱乐新闻稿报道歌手杜德伟(Alex To)如何摆脱伤病重拾信心,开启"Get Up 起来"世界巡回演唱会,初稿标题是:"Alex To 'Gets Up' again and back on stage from adversity"。为了让标题更抓眼,笔者从凑韵的角度思考,定稿标题改为"Alex To: From pain to gain, back on stage again"。

曾任英国老牌杂志《旁观者》(*The Spectator*)总编辑的英国前首相约翰逊使用头韵修辞也是驾轻就熟。《经济学人》"The rise of unpopulism"一文开篇第一段便从约翰逊巧用头韵构词谈起,请看:

> Boris Johnson's attack had an *alliterative* snap. At the despatch box, the prime minister dismissed Sir Keir Starmer, Labour's chief and a former barrister, as "a lawyer, not a leader". The line had one flaw: beyond Westminster, lawyers are liked. (February 12, 2022)

约翰逊讽刺反对党党魁基尔·斯塔默(Keir Starmer)是"a lawyer, not a leader"。《经济学人》很敏锐地注意到"lawyer"与"leader"的头韵修辞(/l/ 音),并以此做文章,也用头韵回敬:lawyers are liked。

头韵修辞藏着编辑的文思,读者若是"视而不见",会错过很多乐趣。把前后两处头韵(/l/ 音)分别译成中文,尤其是第二句

"lawyers are liked"，传递文意毫无难度，但再现英文的音韵却不容易。

英文中有很多脍炙人口的固定表达都内含头韵修辞，这并非巧合，而是因为头韵可使文字节奏明快、悦耳易记。比如，"pull the plug on""busy as a bee""neck and neck""right as rain"等。欧美大报大刊编辑部都对头韵青睐有加，也并非巧合。请看《纽约客》文章开篇第一句：

> We have long known that Donald Trump is a font of falsehoods. (*The New Yorker*, August 6, 2023)

"font"一词用得好。"font"的意思是"an abundant source"（《美国传统词典》），把特朗普比作不断喷涌"谎言"的喷泉（fountain），既形象又犀利。同时，"font of falsehoods"有明显的头韵构词考虑（/f/ 音）。开篇第一句既有隐喻又有头韵，这样的文字怎能不招人喜欢？

> TED, the US non-profit famous for snappy speeches from visionary leaders, espouses the belief that there is no greater force for changing the world than an idea. (*Financial Times*, August 9, 2023)

《金融时报》文章开篇第一句里的"snappy speeches"很见编辑文思。在笔者看来，可以拿来修饰 TED 演讲风格的形容词有很多，比如"engaging""inspiring""thought-provoking"等，但"snappy"胜在轻快有力，与"speech"构成头韵（/s/ 音），表达"sharp and to the point"之意。

多多留意外媒写作中的头韵修辞，不但能增加阅读乐趣，也有助于开阔翻译思路，增进英文文采。

美国《时代周刊》报道明星网红"炫富、偷税漏税",在英文构词上有明显的头韵考虑。请看:

So far, celebrities who <u>flaunt their wealth and welch on taxes</u> have found themselves abruptly taken off the internet. (*Time*, September 8, 2021)

《时代周刊》没有把"偷税漏税"翻译成更常见的"evade/dodge taxes",而是用了一个贬义色彩很浓的非正式词汇"welch",与"wealth"凑头韵(/w/ 音)的意图十分明显。

welch: (informal *disapproving*) to avoid doing something you have promised to do, especially not to pay a debt (《剑桥高级学习词典》)

读者要注意:在新闻写作或者非正式语境,"welch on taxes"不失为一种生动的表达,但是,动词"welch"是"welsh"的变体,这个词可能令"威尔士人(Welsh)"感到冒犯。因此,英译严肃的时政文本,笔者不建议借用"welch"一词来翻译"偷税漏税"。

《时代周刊》翻译"偷税漏税"的选词考量给我们一点启示:头韵修辞在英汉互译中是有用武之地的,必要时我们不妨从这个思路构词。先看一例汉译英:

我国工人阶级和广大劳动群众要……<u>勤学苦练、深入钻研</u>,勇于创新、敢为人先,不断提高技术技能水平,为推动高质量发展、实施制造强国战略、全面建设社会主义现代化国家贡献智慧和力量。(习近平致首届大国工匠创新交流大会的贺信,2022-4-27)

翻译的难点是这四组词：勤学苦练、深入钻研、勇于创新、敢为人先。在这个语境下，为确保译文流畅达意，这四组词不能翻译得太过冗长复杂，可考虑选取四个英文名词与之对应，并以头韵构词。请看：

> With diligence, dedication, innovation and initiative, they should keep honing their skills and contribute their wisdom and strength to promoting high-quality development, making China strong in manufacturing, and building a modern socialist country in all respects.

反过来，翻译英文里的头韵，也可以借用汉语中的修辞手法，比如对偶。例如，2017年，特朗普曾向朝鲜放狠话：

> They will be met with fire and fury like the world has never seen.

"fire and fury"就用了头韵修辞（/f/ 音），"fire"象征"武器或力量（weapons or force）"，"fury"指"愤怒（anger）"。不妨考虑用两个四字成语来翻译"fire and fury"，还原英文的音韵和气势：(他们将承受前所未有的)雷霆之击、雷霆之怒。

小小头韵，大有用途，不可小视。

1.3.2 "凑三"规则

除了在选词上"凑韵"，英文新闻写作还常常借助"凑三"规则（Rule of Three），给文字增加一点节奏，让文字多一分穿透力。

路透社新闻标题"How 2022 *shocked, rocked* and *rolled* global markets"（December 23, 2022）连用三个动词，若只留其一或其二并不影响句意，但"shock""rock""roll"三者并用，节奏感强。

认识新闻写作中的"凑三"规则，不妨读读BBC一篇报道的开篇两段，讲的是凯文·麦卡锡历尽投票波折终于如愿当选美国众议院议长：

It took 15 ballots, a midnight vote and a near-fistfight in the hallowed chambers of Congress, but Kevin McCarthy has now been elected Speaker of the House of Representatives.

Through a combination of cajoling, arm-twisting and finger-jabbing, the California congressman succeeded in convincing enough of the 20 holdout Republicans to support him. (BBC, January 7, 2023)

"凑三"规则似乎有一股魔力，给英文表达赋能。少一分则不足，多一分则累赘，唯"三"恰到好处。无论是外媒编辑部还是欧美政客的写作班子，都对"凑三"情有独钟。"凑三"的成分可以是单词或短语。比如：

After that Mr McCarthy began assiduously courting his detractors with glad-handing, backslapping and prodigious fundraising. (*The Economist*, January 4, 2023)

"Location, location, location."（房地产公司常用广告词）

Life, Liberty and the pursuit of Happiness.（美国《独立宣言》）

Government of the people, by the people, for the people, shall not perish from the earth.（林肯《葛底斯堡演说》）

也可以句子"凑三"，比如：

Generations of Americans have responded with a simple creed that sums up the spirit of a people: Yes, we can. Yes, we can. Yes, we can. (2008年奥巴马胜选演说)

《纽约时报》报道美国前总统特朗普被刑事起诉，以三句长度相仿的短句开篇，制造排比，节奏感强，令读者忍不住想朗读出来。请看：

He will be fingerprinted. He will be photographed. He may even be handcuffed. (*The New York Times*, March 30, 2023)

"凑三"的成分应尽量匀称协调，如此方能制造节奏。比如，在上述 BBC 文章中，"15 ballots""a midnight vote""a near-fistfight"都是名词结构，"cajoling""arm-twisting""finger-jabbing"三个词都是"ing"结构。若成分凌乱失调，则非但无法制造节奏，反而破坏句子的流畅性（flow）。谨记这一点，也有益于我们在翻译工作中改进译文。举一个笔者审校的案例：

截至 2022 年底，拥有输配电线路 6,734 公里，发电装机容量 3,052 兆瓦，全年售电量 99.41 亿度。

By the end of 2022, it had 6,734 km of transmission and distribution lines, 3,052 MW installed capacity and the total electricity sales reached 9.941 TWh.（初译）

原文列举了输配电线路里程、发电装机容量以及全年售电量三个数据。初译文在前两个数据上都处理成了名词结构，到了第三个数据却突然变换成短句"sales reached"，读来有些突兀。初译文虽然译出了原文的意思，但在句子节奏方面仍有优化的空间。试修改如下：

By the end of 2022, the company had <u>a total of</u> 6,734 km of transmission and distribution lines, <u>an installed capacity of</u> 3,052 MW, and <u>an electricity sales volume of</u> 9.941 TWh.

这迷人多娇的"Rule of Three"，令无数文字工作者爱不释手！究其原因，大概"凑三"有三大优点：

节奏明快，悦耳易记；
重点突出，扣人心弦；
结构清晰，赏心悦目。

无论是在英文写作还是在中译英实践中，巧用"凑三"规则将会给文字增色不少。

Detail is interesting only if it is relevant.

– Somerset Maugham

1.4 细节

笔者读外媒，特别关注文字里的"细节（detail）"，因为细节中藏着写作者的专业素养与写作态度。新闻写作中的细节处理，表现形式丰富多样，但目的大致有三个：（1）文字明晰（clarity），设身处地为读者阅读方便着想；（2）营造画面，给文字增加一点色彩（color），增强阅读体验；（3）紧扣主题，有的放矢（relevant），与读者共情。

1.4.1 受众意识

做到第一点，写作者首先要建立明确的受众意识。作为大众媒体，顾名思义，面向的读者是具有一般知识水平的大众，这是"底线思维"。大众读者里虽不乏某个题材的行家里手，但媒体编辑部不能假定广大读者都是该题材的专家。比如，外交部声明中常用一个专业词汇"démarche（交涉）"：

China firmly opposes and sternly condemns this, and has made serious démarche and strong protest to the United States.

中方对此坚决反对，严厉谴责，已向美方提出严正交涉和强烈抗议。（外交部官网，2022-8-2）

然而，外媒提到外交词汇"démarche"，一般要用简单英文解释一下这个词的内涵，因为不能假定广大英文读者都深谙外交话语。比如：

On the heels of U.S. Secretary of State Anthony Blinken concluding his visit to China, the country issued a démarche, which is an official complaint filed by one country against another, to U.S. Ambassador Nicholas Burns' office, U.S. officials told the Journal. (*Forbes*, June 22, 2023)

外媒与外交部面向的受众不同，因此外媒即便"照抄"外交部用词，也不能忘记关照读者，这是新闻写作力求"文字明晰（clarity）"的必然要求。

CNN报道中国将新型冠状病毒感染从"乙类甲管"调整为"乙类乙管"，措辞处处关照英文读者：

Since 2020, China has classified Covid as a Category B infectious disease but treated it as a Category A disease, putting it on par with bubonic plague or cholera.

Now, it will be treated as a Category B disease, in the same category as HIV and bird flu. (CNN, December 26, 2022)

CNN 编辑部以鼠疫、霍乱为参照，让英文读者感知"乙类甲管"的防控等级。这句"classified Covid as a Category B infectious disease but treated it as a Category A disease"只是完成了中文的字面翻译，让读者读懂的"最后一公里"尚未打通。同理，以艾滋病、禽流感为参照，让英文读者感知"乙类乙管"的防控等级，方便读者感知防控措施的调整。CNN 面向的主要读者并非熟知中国传染病防控的专家，若不增添细节信息，一般读者见到"Category B/A"一定会迷茫。

路透社报道中提到专业的医疗器械"血氧仪"，也并不满足于照搬"oximeter"这一专业术语，而是用了简明英语稍加阐释，让读者一目了然。请看：

> China's National Health Commission has said it would equip every village clinic with pulse oximeters, fingertip devices commonly used during the pandemic to quickly check oxygen levels. (Reuters, January 16, 2023)

外媒编辑部对读者"无微不至"的关照，值得国际传播工作者学习效仿，尤其在对外宣介中国特色概念、传统文化符号时。比如，把"三甲公立医院"翻译成"a Class 3A public hospital"，只是完成了翻译任务，还未走完对外传播"最后一公里"。不妨补上几个词"a Class 3A (the highest grade in China) public hospital"，让读者对"Class 3A"在中国医院评级系统中的地位有个认识。同理，把"北京发布高温红色预警"翻译成"Beijing issued a red alert for high temperatures"还不够。请看路透社的表述：

Beijing upgraded its hot weather warning on Friday to "red", the highest in its colour-coded alert system. (Reuters, June 23, 2023)

外媒在报道"神舟（Shenzhou）""天河（Tianhe）"等航天项目时，常常不吝笔墨给拼音"Shenzhou""Tianhe"作注。

In the latest iteration of Shenzhou, which means "Divine Craft," ... (Bloomberg)

The spacecraft, Shenzhou-16, or "Divine Vessel", ... (Reuters)

Tianhe, "Harmony of the Heavens", ... (Reuters)

古人把银河称为"天河"，"神舟"既与"神州（Divine Land）"谐音，又承载着天河行舟的梦想。在拼音"Shenzhou""Tianhe"后面补充英文释义并非必须，但也绝非画蛇添足。把富含传统文化内涵的航天项目名称转换成拼音而不做任何英文阐释，未免有些可惜。广大英文读者单从拼音中其实丝毫领略不到名称的文化魅力。

在对外传播实践中，拼音有其用武之地，但也要认识到它的局限性。有时候，一"拼"了之，自己看似省事，真正的受众却懵了。若要兼顾中国文化的"符号性"与"传播性"，我们在对外报道中不妨学习路透社与彭博社的表达方法，拼音之外，该阐释的时候莫要吝啬键盘。这算一条"中庸"之道。唯其中庸，方能行稳致远。

中文稿中常见"十八大以来"这一表达，转换成英文最好补上时间细节（"since the 18th CPC National Congress in 2012"），目的是让广大英文读者有个清晰的时间坐标。英文报道中提到中国的城市，一般会以英文读者比较熟悉的符号作参照，比如：

<u>in the industrial city of Shijiazhuang, 300 km (185 miles) south-west of Beijing</u>. (*The Economist*, December 18, 2019)

Zhengzhou, the industrial capital of a province of about 100mn people and <u>home to the world's largest Apple iPhone factory</u> (*Financial Times*, July 10, 2023)

外媒新闻标题中提到非英语国家领导人时常常标明国家，比如：

<u>Japan PM</u> Kishida unveils economic action plan on 'new capitalism' (Reuters, June 6, 2023)

<u>Brazil's</u> Lula says he received letter from <u>China's</u> Xi on further cooperation (Reuters, January 3, 2023)

有意思的是，外媒提到英美国家领导人，几乎不会添加"America's""Britain's"，因为外媒默认英美国家领导人在英文世界是家喻户晓的。这一语言现象背后是话语格局的体现，值得读者观察。

1.4.2 营造画面

富含色彩与画面的镜头语言更有感染力和穿透力，因为镜头语言更直接，一个动作或者一个眼神都可能令人动容。相比而言，文字语言若要感染读者，得先在读者脑海中营造画面，这十分考验写作者的功力，需要写作者具有一定的想象力，懂得在文字细节处勾勒画面。

BBC报道一则社会"奇闻"：一头老鹰叼着一条蛇飞行，不慎将蛇掉落，正巧掉在64岁的佩吉·琼斯（Peggy Jones）手臂上，蛇缠住手臂并攻击佩吉的脸，老鹰俯冲下来欲夺回猎物，用鹰爪抓伤了佩吉手臂。请看BBC如何描述这一细节：

> Peggy Jones, 64, was mowing her lawn last month when a passing hawk dropped a snake on her before <u>swooping down</u> to <u>angrily try</u> to reclaim its meal. The snake <u>wrapped itself around her arm</u> and began striking her face as the bird <u>sunk its talons deep into her flesh</u>. (BBC, August 9, 2023)

短短两句话，通过"swoop""wrap around""strike""sink into"等具体而形象的动词，给读者还原了佩吉同时被一头老鹰和一条蛇攻击的画面。可怜的佩吉，真是祸不单行！

英文小说里不乏生动的细节描摹，高明的小说家能以寥寥数笔勾勒出一个个鲜活立体的人物。请看小说《加勒比海盗》主人公杰克船长第一次出场时的描写：

> His <u>tricornered hat jauntily</u> atop his head, revealing the hint of a <u>red bandanna</u> beneath. When he smiled, the sun <u>glinted</u> off his several <u>gold teeth</u>. On almost every one of his fingers <u>flashed</u> a ring, and bits of silver and other trinkets hung from his <u>brown, dreadlocked hair</u>.

三角帽、红色头巾、金牙、满手的戒指、褐色发辫上形形色色的小饰品，配合"glint""flash"这种光线感十足的动词，短短三句话，杰克船长那邪魅不羁的形象便跃然纸上。

新闻英语虽有别于文学作品，但也离不开细节的描摹，尤其在以人物为报道对象时。大而虚的抽象表达一般难以触动读者心弦，精而细的具体描摹更容易令读者回味。

《经济学人》给电影《夺宝奇兵5：命运转盘》写影评，开篇第一句便画面感十足：

> We saw the whip – and saw him use it – before we saw his face, Harrison Ford's rugged features perspiring beneath that battered fedora. (*The Economist*, June 29, 2023)

哈里森·福特饰演的印第安纳·琼斯博士给几代影迷留下深刻印象，《经济学人》开篇便以"鞭子、软呢帽、粗犷的脸庞"这三个元素勾勒经典画面，可谓深谙读者心思。如今，80岁高龄的哈里森再续经典，当他戴着标志性软呢帽、挥舞着鞭子再现荧屏，全球无数影迷激动落泪。

路透社报道超级富豪投资新加坡，通过一段衣着描摹，让读者感受到财富的冲击。请看：

> The forum at Singapore's Shangri-La hotel was attended by hundreds of wealthy people, many bedecked in designer gear from Hermes belt buckles to monogrammed Gucci shawls and the latest Dior bags. (Reuters, January 31, 2023)

爱马仕皮带扣、古驰字母提花围巾、最新款迪奥包……通过具体到品牌的细节描摹，营造出满满的画面感。你是否感受到一股奢华气息扑面而来？

美国诗人罗伯特·弗洛斯特（Robert Frost）说，写作者感动不了自己，就感动不了读者（No tears in the writer, no tears in the reader.）。细节描摹亦是如此：写作者脑中没有画面，又怎能在读者脑中勾勒出画面？

No image in the writer's head, no image in the reader's head.

1.4.3 有的放矢

唐代诗人白居易说过，"文章合为时而著，歌诗合为事而作"。写文章须有的放矢，忌无病呻吟。新闻写作中的细节描摹也要"为时""为事"而作，要与主题相得益彰，否则就成了东拼西凑滥竽充数，毫无意义。

外媒报道乌克兰总统泽连斯基，总会不失时机地描摹一下他的衣着，比如《卫报》：

Zelenskiy – who was dressed in a black fleece, khaki trousers and desert boots – said compromise ... was currently impossible. (*The Guardian*, February 24, 2023)

泽连斯基身穿黑色抓绒外套、卡其裤，脚穿一双沙漠靴，称（与俄罗斯）妥协是不可能的。

俄乌危机爆发以来，泽连斯基有意以"衣着"明志。他曾对英国《金融时报》记者克里斯托弗·米勒（Christopher Miller）表示，乌克兰得胜之前，自己不再穿西装、打领带。《卫报》特地描写泽连斯基的"战斗风"着装，实际上与有声的表态（said compromise ... impossible）形成组合拳，表达不妥协的决心。

细读外媒，总能发现关于泽连斯基衣着的细节描写，比如"wear an olive green T-shirt or jumper（身穿橄榄绿短袖或毛衣）""khaki colored trousers / cargo trousers（卡其色军裤或者工装裤）""brown boots（棕色靴子）"，等等。这既是给文章增色，更是为了与主题契合。

2023年7月8日，国务院副总理、中美经贸中方牵头人何立峰在京会见美财政部长耶伦（Janet L. Yellen）。《华盛顿邮报》在报道中特地"插入"一句会晤场地描写——"在有八盏方形吊灯点亮的挑高会客厅中举行"：

> Saturday's talks – held in a high-ceiled room lit by eight square chandeliers – included other fresh faces on the Chinese side of the table, including Pan Gongsheng, the incoming central bank chief. (*The Washington Post*, July 8, 2023)

《华盛顿邮报》在文字中加入"挑高会客厅""八盏方形吊灯"这一细节描述，有何目的？笔者让基于大语言模型GPT-4的Bing GPT来解答一下。

问：What's the purpose of adding this part "– held in a high-ceiled room lit by eight square chandeliers –"?

Bing GPT: The purpose of adding this part is to provide some descriptive details about the setting of the talks. It helps the reader to imagine the scene and the atmosphere of the meeting. It also suggests that the talks were held in a formal and luxurious place, which may imply the importance or the tension of the negotiations.

看来人工智能是懂新闻写作的，它的回答很周全。此处插入场地细节描摹的目的有两个：（1）给文字增加画面感，方便读者想象会晤场景与气氛；（2）通过描写会晤场地的严肃与气派，间接反映此次会晤的重要性。

这句细节描摹虽非必须，但反映出写作者对细节的关注。文字"走深走细"，才容易抓住读者的心，粗线条的文字往往寡淡如水，难以入脑入心。中英文都是如此。

2023年1月，美国前财政部长拉里·萨默斯（Larry Summers）接受美国彭博社连线采访时表示，失业率增长对控制通胀是必要的。这一言论遭到美国网民批评。美国保守派媒体《纽约邮报》在报道中不失时机地添加细节，悄无声息地撩拨读者情绪。请看文章关键一段：

> The former Treasury Secretary, now a Harvard University professor as well as a paid contributor to Bloomberg News, appeared on Bloomberg's "Wall Street Week" wrap-up news show on Friday, appearing relaxed in a white button-down shirt while reclining in a chair. (*New York Post*, January 9, 2023)

拉里·萨默斯如今是哈佛大学教授、彭博社特约评论员，身份显赫，毫无疑问属于社会精英阶层，与生计无着的失业群体形成鲜明对比。更甚者，萨默斯接受连线专访时，正在风景如画的热带海边度假，身着休闲衬衫，斜坐在椅子上，好不惬意。

《纽约邮报》刻意凸显萨默斯的显赫身份与慵懒姿态，让"失业率增长对控制通胀是必要的"这一言论更加刺耳，给人"何不食肉糜"的既视感。这一细节描摹又与文章标题相呼应：

Larry Summers blasted for hailing US job losses from 'tropical paradise'

好一个"热带天堂（tropical paradise）"！平民百姓听到这位民主党精英的评论，怎能不怒发冲冠？

新闻写作中的细节描摹，无论是衣着描写还是神态刻画，要做到有的放矢，要与文章主旨相得益彰，起到锦上添花的作用。如果细节描摹不能呼应文章主旨，纯粹为了细节而细节，那样的细节描摹就成了"老太太的裹脚布"了。

Don't tell me the moon is shining; show me the glint of light on broken glass.

– Anton Chekhov

1.5 修辞

读外媒，品读修辞手法是一大乐趣，也是一大难关。外媒常用的修辞手法有隐喻（metaphor）、明喻（simile）、夸张（hyperbole）、用典（allusion）、转喻（metonymy）等等。

相对而言，隐喻修辞使用频率最高。英文中很多表达都带有隐喻的思维方式，有的比较明显，有的比较隐晦，人们甚至已经忽略了某些用词的隐喻属性。

1.5.1 隐喻

毫不夸张地说，隐喻表达在外媒报道中无处不在。读者留言说阅读英美报刊感到吃力，在笔者看来，很大原因是不熟悉英文表达中那些或明或暗的隐喻修辞。

隐喻表达一般有两个优点：一是使文字形象生动，增强文章的可读性；二是言简意赅，有"言有尽而意无穷"之功效。

路透社描述"北约持续加强同亚太国家军事联系",用词不拘一格,形象生动:

> A joint statement included familiar accusations against the West – that the United States was undermining global stability and NATO barging into the Asia-Pacific region. (Reuters, March 22)

以"barge into"表达"北约突兀地闯进亚太地区"显然是隐喻用法,这一隐喻用法与驳船有关(rough handling of barges)。"barge"既可作名词,表示"大型平底驳船",也可作动词,意思是"to intrude or interrupt, especially rudely"(《美国传统词典》)。路透社用动词"barge"这样一个冲击力十足的动词描述北约,给读者留下深刻印象。当然也可以用"intrude"替换"barge",仍能传递出"北约不受欢迎"的感情色彩,但二者的"词气"略有不同。"barge"比"intrude"更形象生动,多一分鲁莽蛮横。这是外媒编辑部选词的逻辑。

亚里士多德说,善用隐喻是聪明才智的体现,因为善用隐喻者有一双发现事物相似性的眼睛。英国前首相约翰逊曾把新冠病毒比作行凶的"暴徒",鼓励人们团结起来把"暴徒"摔倒在地:

> If this virus were a physical assailant, an unexpected and invisible mugger, which I can tell you from personal experience it is, then this is the moment we have begun together to wrestle it to the floor. (April 27, 2020)

新冠疫情初期,人们面对病毒难免有担忧与恐慌,"阳康"后的约翰逊把病毒比作"assailant/mugger",虽然有把复杂问题简单化的倾向，但这番画面感和幽默感十足的话，无疑提振了民众战胜病毒的决心与信心。

英文新闻写作有一个重要的选词思路，即，选词用词要有意识地向着文章主题靠拢，笔者概括为"到什么山头唱什么歌"。《华盛顿邮报》报道印度电动汽车产业，文内有这样一句隐喻表达：

> The economics, though, is exactly why four-wheeled EVs are likely to have a bumpy ride in India. (*The Washington Post*, January 19, 2023)

由"四轮电动车"想到"have a ride"顺理成章，以"have a bumpy ride（前路颠簸）"喻"发展前景充满挑战（a difficult or challenging situation）"也是顺理成章。报道汽车产业，记者编辑很容易想到"gear up""rev up""switch gears"等由汽车引申出来的隐喻表达。同理，《经济学人》报道"淄博烧烤热"，选词用词也体现了"到什么山头唱什么歌"的思路。请看：

> *National statistics, grilled*
>
> The meaty mystery at the heart of China's economic growth (May 11, 2023)

副标题里的动词"grill"最常用的意思是"烧烤"，引申开来表达"analyze closely"之意。主标题里的形容词"meaty"也是满满烧烤味儿，意思是：prompting considerable thought（《美国传统词典》）。

"grill"与"meaty"都是隐喻用法，都是围绕"烧烤"这一主题的"严选"之词,既切题又增色。试想,若是把"meaty"替换成同义词"thought-provoking",就太无趣了。

除了让文字形象生动,隐喻表达常常言简义丰,因而备受中外作家青睐。美国诗人查尔斯·布考斯基(Charles Bukowski)对杜甫和李白"言简义丰"的用字艺术钦佩有加:

> ... the early Chinese poets like Tu Fu and Li Po who could say more in one line than most could say in thirty or ever. (*Essential Bukowski: Poetry*,《布考斯基精选诗集》)

隐喻是诗歌语言意象性的一个重要手段。李白和杜甫常常在诗中隐喻个人前途与国家命运,意境深邃悠远,回味无穷,正如布考斯基所言"say more in one line than most could say in thirty or ever"。

法国历史学家费尔南·布罗代尔(Fernand Braudel)有句名言,也是精炼的隐喻表达:"La France, c'est la langue française. (France is the French language.)"。《纽约时报》评论文章指出,这句话完美表达了"狂热的语言沙文主义(overzealous linguistic chauvinism)"(*The New York Times*, August 8, 2023)。"法国就是法语""时间就是金钱""江山就是人民"等,都是凝练的隐喻表达。一句话可以省却千言万语,令人回味。《经济学人》谈"美国经济衰退论",开篇第一句便是隐喻表达,短短7个单词,却词尽意不尽。请看:

> American economic declinism is a broad church. Voices on the right claim that big government has *stifled* the frontier spirit and that soaring debt has condemned future generations to poverty. The left worries that inequality and corporate power have *hollowed* out the economy. (April 13, 2023)

"美国经济衰退论是一座大教堂",此话何解?先来看"broad church"的词典释义:

a group, organization, or set of beliefs that includes <u>a wide range of different opinions or ideas</u>(《剑桥高级学习词典》)

以"a broad church"作喻,三个词却道出两层意思:"美国经济衰退论"有广泛的支持者;更重要的是,支持者中观点也并不统一,视角多元,好似宗教里的派系林立。二三句则顺理成章地进一步展开,介绍美国右派(the right)和左派(the left)虽然都认为美国经济在衰退,但各有各的解读。第三句中的"*hollowed out the economy*(掏空经济)"又是隐喻表达。如果算上第二句里的"*stifle* the spirit",短短三句话便内含三处隐喻表达。隐喻修辞与思维方式、传统习俗息息相关,读者若是不熟悉英文写作中的隐喻修辞,读起来一定倍感吃力。

从外媒文字中领略形形色色的隐喻表达,发现不同事物之间潜在的相似性,在品读隐喻中打磨英文隐喻思维,也是一件快乐事。

1.5.2 用典

英文中不少典故已为国人耳熟能详,比如"丘比特之箭(Cupid's arrow)""阿喀琉斯之踵(Achilles' heel)""达摩克利斯之剑(the Sword of Damocles)"。面对同一文化背景的读者,用典既可以增加文采,又能引起文化共鸣,拉近距离。

外媒用典多从希腊神话以及英文文学经典中取材。路透社报道七国集团峰会,以希腊神话开篇,请看:At one point in Homer's

Odyssey, the hero has to steer his ship between twin dangers: Scylla, a multi-headed monster, and the whirlpool of Charybdis. Leaders of the Group of Seven rich countries meeting this month in Hiroshima may feel they are in a similar situation...（Reuters, May 8, 2023）

在希腊神话中，墨西拿海峡（the Strait of Messina）两侧，一边是恐怖的海妖斯库拉（Scylla），一边是凶险的漩涡卡律布狄斯（Charybdis）。英文谚语"between Scylla and Charybdis"常用来比喻"两面受敌、进退两难"。

英美政客演讲经常引用莎士比亚名言。2022年9月1日，美国总统拜登在费城发表题为"Soul of the Nation"的演讲。在演讲中，拜登把特朗普及其支持者"MAGA Republicans"（即"make America great again" Republicans）称为"极端分子"，称他们对美国立国之基构成威胁。演讲结尾，拜登引用莎翁名句呼吁选民捍卫立国之基：

> And if we all do our duty – if we do our duty in 2022 and beyond, then ages still to come will say we – all of us here – we kept the faith. We preserved democracy.

这句古色古香的英文"ages still to come will say"化用了莎士比亚十四行诗（第17首）里的句子：

> The age to come would say 'This poet lies; ...'
> 后人会说"诗人撒谎……"。

换成现代英语里的大白话就是"the future generations will say"，但"ages still to come will say"更富文采。《经济学人》尤

其擅长从文学典故中取材，用典有时比较明显，有时比较隐蔽。先看明着用典的两个例子：

> It was among nearly 20 measures he introduced that favoured either him or his businesses, which grew like Topsy while he was in power. (*The Economist*, June 12, 2023)

本段出自《经济学人》为意大利前总理贝卢斯科尼撰写的讣告。Topsy 是经典小说《汤姆叔叔的小屋》里的黑人小女孩。当别人问她是否听过上帝，是否知道自己从哪儿来，她笑着回答："I spect I grow'd. Don't think nobody never made me."。

"grow like Topsy" 进入现代英语，表达"疯长"之意：

> grow very fast, particularly in an unplanned or uncontrolled way (thefreedictionary.com)

贝卢斯科尼主政期间，名下商业帝国迅猛发展，《经济学人》编辑部用"grew like Topsy"一方面给文字增加文采，另一方面比单纯使用"grew rapidly"多了一层"without regulation"的暗示，因为一系列利好政策都是自己主政时制定的。

> Today, however, Republicans espouse a Goldilocks principle of government, says Bennett Sandlin, the head of the Texas Municipal League, an advocacy group. "The federal government is big and bad, cities are small and bad, and somehow state government gets it just right." (*The Economist*, June 3, 2023)

"Goldilocks principle（金发姑娘原则）",源自英国经典童话故事《三只小熊》。金发女孩误闯熊屋,趁主人未归,品尝了三碗粥、试坐了三把椅子、试躺了三张床,发现粥不太冷也不太热是最好的,床和椅子不太大也不太小才最舒服。"金发姑娘原则"就是"执其两端用其中"。在本段语境下,美国共和党在"联邦政府""州政府""(基层)市政府"三者中更看重"州政府",因为联邦政府太大,市政府太小,州政府不大不小正合适。

再看《经济学人》"暗戳戳"用典的一例:

Two wheels good

Forget Teslas, India's EV revolution is happening on two wheels. (*The Economist*, April 20, 2023)

《经济学人》这篇文章谈印度电动车产业革命,中心思想是:引领产业革命的不是四轮电动汽车,而是两轮电动踏板车、摩托车。副标题"Two wheels good"暗中模仿乔治·奥威尔政治讽喻小说《动物庄园》(*Animal Farm*)里的口号。

在小说中,猪率领群畜把农场主赶跑,建立了动物自治的乐园,并旗帜鲜明地喊出一句口号:

Four legs good, two legs bad.

猪还率领群畜定下七条戒律:

凡两条腿走路的,皆为敌;
凡四条腿走路或长翅膀的,皆为友;
不准穿衣;

不准睡床；

不准喝酒；

不准相互残害；

众畜平等。

可惜，后来猪变质了，没有抵抗住人类的"糖衣炮弹"，带头把七条戒律一一打破。于是，口号一夜之间发生变化：

Four legs good, two legs better!

副标题里的"Two wheels good"便是化用了小说里的口号，与文章主旨十分契合：引领印度产业革命的是两轮电动车。

我们读外媒，若是见到"Two wheels good"匆匆读过而不知其所以然，恐怕会错过用典之乐。若照字面把"Two wheels good"翻译出来，中文读者更不太可能感受此中乐趣。

1.5.3 转喻等其他修辞

外媒写作还常用转喻（metonymy）修辞。《美国传统词典》这样解释转喻：

A figure of speech in which one word or phrase is substituted for another with which it is closely associated.

新闻英语中，转喻的例子有很多，比如：

以"Washington"指代"the US government"；
以"Beijing"指代"the Chinese government"；
以"Hollywood"指代"the US film industry"；
以"the Kremlin"指代"the Russian government"；
以"the Pentagon"指代"the US Department of Defense"；
以"mercury"指代"temperature"；
……

对新闻编辑部而言，简化用词，可节省版面空间，因此转喻修辞使用较频繁。与转喻相近的修辞手法是提喻（synecdoche）。

synecdoche: A figure of speech in which a part is used for the whole, the whole for a part, the specific for the general, the general for the specific, or the material for the thing made from it.（《美国传统词典》）

提喻：一种修辞手法，即，以部分代整体，以整体代部分，以特定代一般，以一般代特定，或以物体的材质代物体本身。

略举几例：

all hands on deck (hands 代表 sailors)；
hungry mouths to feed (mouths 代表 people)；
I got a new set of wheels. (wheels 代表 car)；
But if Israel's lurch from liberal values continues it will endanger prosperity. Its coders, capitalists and creatives may

move elsewhere. (*The Economist*, April 27, 2023)

《经济学人》文章分析以色列国内的价值观转向，即从自由主义价值观转向右翼保守主义。如果任由这种转向持续下去，不但不利于经济繁荣，而且会导致人才流失。以"coders, capitalists, creatives"这三类特定群体代指以色列各类英才（all kinds of talented people）"，便是运用了"以偏代全"的提喻修辞。若是把这句英文译成中文，三个词可以照字面直译，但最好增补"等各类人才"，才符合英文原意。

另外，"coders, capitalists, creatives"三个词在选词上有明显的头韵修辞考虑，这是《经济学人》典型的新闻写作方式。

明喻（simile）也是外媒常用的修辞手法，使用得当可给文章增色。比如：

Once Omicron gets going, it <u>burns</u> through a population <u>like a forest fire</u>. (*The Economist*, December 7, 2022)

It sounded <u>like</u> a freight train, <u>like</u> a tornado, <u>like</u> rolling thunder – and then a gigantic boom. (*The New York Times*, February 2, 2003)

"拟人（personification）"修辞也散见于外媒报道。比如《卫报》报道中美关系：

Unlike Trump, who is running again for president, the Biden administration has said it is willing to work with China on narrow areas of cooperation such as climate – <u>as Beijing sweats in record mid-June temperatures</u>. (*The Guardian*, June 17, 2023)

六月中旬的北京持续高温，"as Beijing sweats（北京流汗）"这句拟人表达既是描述现实，也在间接强调中美携手应对气候变化的紧迫性。运用拟人修辞比干巴巴地写"as mid-June temperatures soar to new records in Beijing"更易给读者留下深刻印象。

《金融时报》报道中国大学生就业情况，开篇第一句便用拟人修辞抓住读者：

> Job opportunities scream from posters at an employment fair in central China's Zhengzhou... But many of the jobs require 70 hours of work a week and command salaries as low as RMB3,000 ($400) a month. Wang, a commerce graduate, struggles to get enthused.

动词"scream（尖叫）"给文字增添一抹幽默色彩，仿佛招聘海报在呼喊着毕业生"快点看过来"。然而，就业岗位的薪酬和工作时长却让毕业生难以提起兴趣（struggles to get enthused），前后两句形成鲜明反差。如此生动的开场，怎能不勾起读者继续读下去的欲望？

在英文新闻写作中，修辞手法的使用也遵循"金发姑娘原则"，使用太频繁未免显得花里胡哨，但"零修辞"的文字显得干瘪乏味。不多不少，间隔适当，才是最好的。

所谓"内行看门道，外行看热闹"。我们读外媒，不能只满足于收集生词短语，而要学会以"编辑部视角"品句法，品用词，品修辞，品细节。要知其然，知其所以然，读懂外媒的写作逻辑，我们才能举一反三，学以致用。

荀子曰：道虽迩，不行不至；事虽小，不为不成。品读外媒话语风格，需持之以恒，也需从小处着手。日积月累，必有收获。

The headline writer is the poet among journalists, stuffing big meaning into small spaces.

– Roy Peter Clark

1.6 标题

对新闻编辑而言，起标题（headline）也许是最耗费心神的一件事。标题"难产"，好比饺子煮好了，却到处找不到蘸醋，想将就但始终不甘心。

标题的重要性不言而喻。正文内容再好，也怕标题起得烂，所谓"酒香也怕巷子深"。好的标题能吸引读者，赢得流量，品之回味无穷。外媒多是私有化媒体，标题关乎流量，流量关乎读者订阅，读者订阅关乎盈利，外媒编辑部在起标题一事上绝不敢草率怠惰。

起标题最忌不清不楚、糊里糊涂，甚至产生歧义。以下两例标题滑稽感十足：

Dr. Ruth to talk about <u>sex with newspaper editors</u>

Legislators hold forum <u>on electric grid</u>

"sex with newspaper editors"与"on electric grid"都是能引起歧义的表达,这样的标题会遭到读者嘲笑。

在对外报道中,我们免不了要参照中文稿进行编译,在起英文标题时尤其要注意:要起好英文标题,必须跳出中文标题的形式羁绊,在把握文章主旨的基础上创造性发挥。举个例子:

要排队去看的"滚滚"它降级了(中文标题)
Popular "Gungun" no longer "endangered"(初稿标题)

中文标题里以"滚滚"指代熊猫,很可爱,对中文读者而言并无阅读障碍,但如果在英文里直接保留"gungun",两个"gun"合在一起,令人不知所云。乍一看,还以为与"枪支"有关呢!修改如下:

Giant pandas "downgraded": a wildlife success story

把标题起得清晰明了,无歧义,不闹笑话,这是基本要求。在此基础上,要努力让标题生动起来,吸引读者眼球。

起标题特别考验编辑结合语境创造性用词的能力。2023年初,"气球事件"搅动中美关系。外媒纷纷予以报道,请看美联社与路透社的标题:

Chinese balloon soars across US; Blinken scraps Beijing trip (Associated Press)

China balloon soaring over U.S. deflates hopes for diplomatic thaw (Reuters)

注意美联社标题中第二个动词"scrap",不用"cancel""postpone"

等词，意在与第一个动词"soar"呼应。

路透社标题中的"deflate"用得很应景，因为"deflate"既可与"balloon"搭配表示"给气球放气"，又可与抽象的"hope/ego"等词搭配，表示"reduce/discourage"之意。围绕"气球事件"，路透社编辑很自然地想到"deflate"一词，这又是"到什么山头唱什么歌"选词思路的体现。

让标题生动起来有很多技巧可循，可巧用双关语、谐音梗等文字游戏（wordplay）。来看几则外媒案例。

《经济学人》报道（中东）黄沙漫天，曾借"sand"一词玩文字游戏，令人印象深刻：

Sand by me

Dust is a growing threat to lives in the Middle East

副标题"sand by me"是在玩谐音梗。从字面上看，文理欠佳的"sand by me"在告诉读者"sand being all around me（被黄沙包围）"。"sand by me"读快了便与"stand by me"音似，文中配上一张沙尘中掩面疾行的路人图片，这"sand by me"就好似一句定风咒语：help/support me。

stand by someone：to continue to support or help someone who is in a difficult situation（《剑桥高级学习词典》）

在新闻标题中玩谐音梗，一定要结合具体语境，否则玩得四不像就尴尬了。英媒中还常见一句谐音梗："It's no yolk.（It's no joke.）"。

"yolk"的意思是"蛋黄"，这句谐音梗常出现在与"egg"相关的文章里。比如《卫报》标题：

  The egg-white craze: it's no yolk

  "It's no yolk."作谐音梗似已司空见惯，几乎成了陈词滥调。不过，写文章若能因地制宜创造性地玩一点文字游戏，会给文章增色不少，也会给读者留下深刻印象。比如，BBC 这则标题"*Purrfect* shots: The man who took 90,000 photos of cats"把"猫的呼噜声（purr）"与"完美（perfect）"两个单词组合成"purrfect"，与文章主题"photos of cat"完美契合。

  在报道中国的题材中，外媒标题中不乏充满奇思妙想的双关语，令人印象深刻。试举两例。

  2021 年 5 月，"长征五号 B 火箭残骸返回地球"一事备受中外关注，有部分外媒炒作残骸可能失控危及地面人群。《大西洋月刊》发表科普文章，安慰读者"莫惊慌"，因为历史上人被残骸击中的概率比遭雷劈还低。标题巧用"fall to pieces"，一语双关，可谓妙极：

  Don't fall to pieces just because China's rocket is (May 7, 2021)

  "fall to pieces"除了字面意义"摔成碎片（break into parts）"之外，还可引申开来描述"（某人）惊慌失措"：

  to become unable to control one's emotions (*Merriam Webster*)

  标题中的"Don't fall to pieces"是在告诉人们"不必惊慌失

措"，结尾"is"后面省略了"falling to pieces"，用其字面意义。整句标题的意思是：不要因为火箭残骸返回地球会摔成碎片就惊慌失措。

2023年上半年，深圳等地出台相关意见和办法，允许街道办事处根据方便群众、布局合理、监管有序的原则划定摊贩经营场所，这意味着不再全面禁止路边摊。请看《经济学人》的标题：

Setting out their stalls
Another comeback for China's street merchants

副标题"setting out their stalls"一语双关，字面意思是"摆出货摊"，同时"set out one's stall"作为固定短语还可表达"亮明立场/态度（决意做某事）"。请看权威词典释义：

to make all the necessary plans or arrangements that you need to achieve something, and show that you are determined to achieve it (*Collins Dictionary*)

to show your intentions or beliefs in a way that is very clear and determined (thefreedictionary.com)

各地放开摆地摊，目的很明确：恢复城市经济活力，拉动经济增长。这则标题把"setting out their stalls"两种用法集于一身，简洁切题、别出心裁，足见编辑功力。若把标题翻译成中文，恐怕不容易再现原文选词的奇思妙想。

除了谐音和双关语，巧用修辞手法，如凑韵、隐喻、拟人，也是外媒编辑部起标题常用的技巧。

2023年夏季，北京出现罕见的连续高温天气，外媒纷纷报道，用词五花八门，既有隐喻也有拟人，好不热闹！请看：

Beijing sizzles with hot weather alert at highest level (Reuters)

路透社用拟声词"sizzle"来形容高温，很形象。煎过香肠、烙过饼的读者估计已经听到"滋滋冒油"的声音。

美国彭博社以"烤箱（oven）"作喻，用动词"bake"表达"热浪烘烤华北大地"：

Beijing temperature hits record 41.8C as heat wave bakes northern China (Bloomberg)

CNN、法新社则用拟人修辞描述"华北/北京汗流浃背"：

Beijing swelters during hottest June day on record (CNN)

Beijing issues highest heat alert as north China swelters (AFP)

以 ChatGPT 为代表的生成式人工智能问世以来，媒体编辑部都感受到了机遇和挑战。在新闻标题的修改润色方面，生成式人工智能大有可为。笔者曾让 Google Bard 润色下面这则标题：

Various kinds of music around world meet in Xi'an via cultural communication (Xinhua, May 15, 2023)

笔者输入的指令是：Refine this news headline to make it more natural, concise and maybe a bit literary.

Google Bard 给出五条备选答案：

Xi'an: a musical melting pot

The sounds of the world converge in Xi'an

Xi'an celebrates cultural diversity through music

Music unites the world in Xi'an

Xi'an: a beacon of cultural exchange

笔者最喜欢第一个。"a musical melting pot"内含头韵和隐喻修辞，比原标题生动凝练了许多。

在润色标题方面，生成式人工智能可以给新闻工作者提供灵感。《纽约时报》把 ChatGPT 比作"随时可以聊、随时能出点主意的朋友（your always available, spitballing friend）"，可谓形象又贴切。相反，标题起不好，很容易引起非议。2019年，CNN 报道英国王室第一个有非裔血统的混血宝宝，文内小标题"How black will the royal baby be?"遭到《新闻周刊》等美国同行批评。CNN 这篇文章提醒人们不要因为英国王室添了非裔混血宝宝就对种族平等之路抱有不切实际的期待。立意很好，但这小标题问"王室宝宝有几成黑？"便有种族歧视之嫌，令很多读者不悦。2021年，《华盛顿邮报》一则评论文章标题遭到福克斯新闻网等美国保守派媒体嘲讽。请看标题：The media treats Biden as badly as – or worse than – Trump. Here's proof（*The Washington Post*, December 3, 2021）。

标题似乎在为拜登打抱不平，暗含这样一种信息：拜登所应当比特朗普获得更多正面报道。有意思的是，这篇文章在社交媒体上被时任白宫办公厅主任罗恩·克莱恩（Ronald Klain）转发后，福克斯新闻网撰稿人乔·孔查（Joe Concha）评论道：这是"年度最搞笑文章之一（one of the most laughable columns of the year）"。

　　标题起得好，同行叫好，读者称赞；标题起得差，同行嘲笑，读者捧喝。起标题，不可儿戏！

第二章 中国时政话语:译路维艰

2.1 时政话语英译

晚清洋务派官员、语言学家马建忠曾提出"善译"说：

一书到手，经营反复，确知其意旨之所在，而又摹写其神情，仿佛其语气，然后心悟神解，振笔而书，译成之文，适如其所译而止，而曾无毫发出入于其间。

"意旨"，即原文的"spirit"；"神情""语气"，即原文的"style"。"善译"说力求同时兼顾原文意旨与文风，自然是更高"译境"，是译者应当追求的理想目标。钱锺书先生认为，"善译"说与国人熟知的"信、达、雅"三字标准相比，无疑是一大进步。一味求雅，可能给原文琐屑之处裹上一层艳丽的外衣。(《钱锺书英文文集》)

"善译"说对英译中国时政话语具有指导意义。一文到手，经营反复，确知其意旨之所在，这是第一步，也是至关重要的一步。准确理解原文，既需要把握好文本本身这一"小语境"，又需要在时政话语风格特点、政治文化这个"大语境"里去探求。

2023 年《政府工作报告》中出现六次"阶段性"，译者必须把握好"小语境"与"大语境"，探查其意旨，不能想当然。

实施大规模减税降费政策，制度性安排与阶段性措施相结合。疫情发生后减税降费力度进一步加大，成为应对冲击的关键举措。

We implemented a policy of large-scale tax and fee cuts with both institutional arrangements and time-limited measures. Tax and fee reductions were intensified following the outbreak of Covid-19, and they became a pivotal part of our response to the epidemic.

疫情期间，各国政府均出台临时性（temporary）纾困解难措施，即"阶段性"措施。请看《经济学人》这段报道：

The Covid-19 pandemic forced governments all over the world to temporarily increase social-welfare programmes... Some states also used the Temporary Assistance for Needy Families (TANF) programme, a federal cash-assistance scheme, to further help vulnerable families. (*The Economist*, March 16, 2023)

在中国时政话语中，"阶段性"除了表"temporary/time-limited"之意，还可表"分阶段/逐步地（in a phased way / in stages）""当前阶段（for the current stage）"之意。译者既要细品上下文，还得勤查政策，才能译对译准。

阶段性将小规模纳税人增值税起征点从月销售额 3 万元提高到 15 万元、小微企业所得税实际最低税负率从 10% 降至 2.5%。

The VAT threshold was raised from 30,000 yuan to 150,000 yuan of monthly sales for small-scale taxpayers in a phased way, and the minimum corporate income tax rate was cut from 10 percent to 2.5 percent in real terms for micro and small businesses.

这句话里的"阶段性"为何不能理解为"temporary"？译者从上下文这一"小语境"中难以觅得答案，需要从政策这一"大语境"中去探查。2019年《政府工作报告》提出：落实好小规模纳税人增值税起征点从月销售额3万元提高到10万元等税收优惠政策。2021年《政府工作报告》提出：将小规模纳税人增值税起征点从月销售额10万元提高到15万元。由此可见，从3万元到15万元，是分阶段实现的，因此"阶段性"乃"分阶段"之意。

巩固和完善农村基本经营制度，完成承包地确权登记颁证和农村集体产权制度改革<u>阶段性</u>任务。

We consolidated and improved the basic rural operation system and completed the work to determine, register, and certify contracted rural land rights and the reform of the rural collective property rights system <u>for the current stage</u>.

译之道最微，微则不得不深究。译者既要能"钻进去"，探查中国时政话语之内里，又得能"跳出来"，对中国时政话语的特点和整体风格有个全面把握，方能识得庐山真面。

历史学家萧功秦先生曾总结中国传统概念的三个基本特点：意会性（非定义性）、模糊性（非确指性）、板块性（不可离析性）。"千百年来生活在以这样一种概念体系为思维手段的文化环境中，人们运用形象而精巧的比喻，同样可以把最深奥复杂的思想，以意会的方式加以表达。……'读时不求甚解，会心在牝牡骊黄之外。'意会性的学习与思维方法，也就这样一代一代地传了下来。"（《儒家文化的困境》）

中国传统概念的三个基本特点在今天的时政话语中依然有深刻的烙印。抽象的表达，模糊的术语，精巧的比喻，修饰词的堆叠，对用典、排比、对仗的执着，既是传统文风照进现代话语，也彰显了鲜明的时代特色。

翻译不是从"0"到"1"的构建，而是某种映射。评价《政府工作报告》等重要时政文件的英译文，若无视中国时政话语的基本特点，单从英文美不美的角度去评判，就好比只看镜花水月，忘记了低头赏花抬头望月。

瑞典汉学家沈迈克（Michael Schoenhals）指出，相比日常话语而言，政治话语在"词语、风格、句法、修辞手法"等方面受到的限制更多。

"The language of politics is a restricted code, one in which options with respect to formal qualities such as vocabulary, style, syntax, and trope are far more restricted than in ordinary language." (*Doing Things with Words in Chinese Politics: Five Studies*)

"restricted code"一词用得到位。笔者对中国时政话语的特点分析就要从这个词说起。

2.1.1 时政话语特点分析

意会性

"限定型语码（restricted code）"是英国社会学家巴兹尔·伯恩斯坦（Basil Bernstein）提出的概念，与之相对的是"精致型语码（elaborate code）"。"限定型语码"依赖具体的语境，对使用者与听者的话语"共识"要求较高，常常"语尽而意远"。相比而言，"精致型语码"不囿于具体语境，对使用者与听者的话语"共识"要求较低，因而措辞精密严谨、阐释充足。英国教育学者詹姆斯·阿瑟顿（James Atherton）对二者的区别解释得最明了：

> The restricted code works better than the elaborated code for situations in which there is a great deal of shared and taken-for-granted knowledge in the group of speakers. It is economical and rich, conveying a vast amount of meaning with a few words, each of which has a complex set of connotations and acts like an index, pointing the hearer to a lot more information which remains unsaid. (*Language Codes*[1])

> 当讲话者之间存在广泛的认知交集，限定型语码比精致型语码更适用。限定型语码言简义丰，寥寥数语即可传递丰富内涵，每个词都蕴含复杂的内涵，好似一个索引，指引听者领会更多未言明之信息。

沈迈克借"限制型语码"这一概念来描述中国时政话语，说明时政话语的受众相对较窄，讲话者与听者之间需要具备一定的话语共识和认知交集。实际上，时政话语中有些提法自诞生以来仅面向特定的受众。最典型的例子就是"韬光养晦"一词。美国学者曾敏锐地注意到这一点：

> This was a phrase that others in leadership positions needed to hear; it did not need mass consumption. (*An*

---

[1] https://www.doceo.co.uk/background/language_codes.htm

Anatomy of Chinese: Rhythm, Metaphor, Politics）

从历史上看，"韬光养晦"这个词一开始就不是讲给广大群众听的，更不是要大张地旗鼓地讲给海外受众。一旦"昭告天下"，不管最后译成"keep a low profile"还是按照外媒习惯译法"hide (your strength) and bide (your time)"，对译法的争论就已经超出翻译本身，变成了对中国外交政策的解读。就好比，一本小说问世，读者如何解读，原作者也无法"一锤定音"。

限定型语码"言简义丰"的特点也意味着，时政话语的概念、范畴及语词体系具有较强的"意会性"，所谓"句中有余味，篇中有余意"。时政话语的"意会性"首先体现在概念层面。

比如，"人类命运共同体"这一概念的外延和内涵伸缩性较大，既可以用在外交领域，比如，中国—中亚命运共同体，也可以用在科技合作、教育、粮食安全、气候变化等诸多领域。《2021中国的航天》白皮书首次提出，在外空领域推动构建人类命运共同体。

美国智库大西洋理事会在2021年发布的一份报告中用"amorphous"一词描述这一概念。

amorphous：having no fixed form or shape（《剑桥高级学习词典》）

笔者在第一章指出，外媒用词力求"具体化"，因为词语越具体，指向性越明确，画面感越强，反之，用词越抽象，给人感觉越朦胧。

日裔美籍语言学家早川一会（S.I. Hayakawa）曾提出"抽象阶梯（Ladder of Abstraction）"的概念。不妨画一个抽象阶梯，自下而上逐渐趋于抽象：

人类

中国人

山东人

济南人

济南一位老师

济南某学校一位老师

济南某学校一位物理老师

济南某学校物理老师张三

从文字层面看,"人类命运共同体"包含两个抽象位阶很高的词——"人类""命运"。美国智库认为这个概念"摸不透"也就不足为奇了。不管翻译如何用力,把它译成"a human community with a shared future"(党的二十大报告)也好,译成更贴近原文原意和英文表达习惯的"a global community of shared future(《中国时政话语翻译基本规范·英文》)"也罢,英文读者看到这样的表述可能还是会忍不住问一句:"What exactly does it mean?"。实际上,中外英文媒体都发表了不少解读"人类命运共同体"的评论文章,目的无非是把这个概念讲清楚、解释透。重要政治概念的对外传播,翻译只是第一步,让概念传得开、叫得响,离不开细致巧妙的解读与阐释。

再比如"(坚持)守正创新"。"正"具体指什么?有学者把"守正"解释为"坚持正确的方向、站稳正确的立场、恪守正确的原则"。还有的学者把"守正"解释为"坚持马克思主义基本原理不动摇,坚持党的全面领导不动摇,坚持中国特色社会主义不动摇。"如此看来,"正"的内涵比较广,非一字一词可以解释清楚。

目前，"守正创新"有两种比较权威的译法：

译法一：maintain the right political orientation and break new ground（《习近平谈治国理政》第四卷英文版）

译法二：uphold fundamental principles and break new ground（党的二十大报告英文版）

"守正"根植于中国传统文化，语出《史记·礼书》："循法守正者见侮于世，奢溢僭差者谓之显荣。"中国传统文化对现代时政话语的影响不容小觑，当有着传统文化烙印的语词体系与现代时政话语交融互动，传统概念本身极强的"意会性"常常给英译工作带来不小的障碍。把"守正创新"四个字译成英文，译者容易陷入"两不讨好"的境地：选词太具体，容易把"正"译窄了；选词太抽象，又容易把"正"译宽了。

中国人的意会性思维特别发达。对于孔子说的"知者乐水，仁者乐山"，"我们每个人都能够凭借自己的理解和想象，赋予这句话更丰富的意义"。（《康辉咬文嚼字》）

当"知者""仁者"等内涵伸缩性较大的传统概念进入今天的政治和外交语境，翻译就成了难点。翻译"知者"，译者要在"wise""knowledgeable""well-informed"等形容词中斟酌；翻译"仁者"，译者要在"virtuous""benevolent"等词中斟酌；"惑"一字究竟译成"doubts"还是"perplexity"，也需要一番思量。译者不得不结合具体语境对传统概念进行再解读、再阐释，没有所谓的万能译法，只有最贴合当下语境的译法。比如：

中国古人说："知者不惑，仁者不忧，勇者不惧。"新形势下，我们要携手构建亚太命运共同体，再创亚太合作新辉煌。（习近平在亚太经合组织第二十九次领导人非正式会议上的讲话，2022–11–18）

As an ancient Chinese sage observed, "The <u>wise</u> are free from <u>perplexity</u>, the <u>virtuous</u> from <u>anxiety</u>, and the <u>brave</u> from <u>fear</u>." Facing the new circumstances, we must join hands together to build an Asia-Pacific community with a shared future and take Asia-Pacific cooperation to a new height.

这里"仁者"之所以译为"virtuous"而非"benevolent",有两个考虑:第一,"benevolent"一词略古旧,根据谷歌全球书籍词频统计器(Google Books Ngram Viewer)统计结果,这个词在19世纪上半叶达到使用高峰,之后使用频率逐渐下降,如今在现代英语中用得很少;第二,在政治语境下,"benevolent"容易给人一种"家长作风(paternalistic)"的等级感,即"上对下的仁慈"。

再比如,当"义利观"进入外交语境:

秉持真实亲诚理念和<u>正确义利观</u>加强同发展中国家团结合作,维护发展中国家共同利益。(党的二十大报告)

Guided by the principles of sincerity, real results, affinity, and good faith and <u>with a commitment to the greater good and shared interests</u>, China endeavors to strengthen solidarity and cooperation with other developing countries and safeguard the common interests of the developing world.

子曰:"君子喻于义,小人喻于利。"朱熹:"义者,事之宜也。"我们似乎很难从传统文献中找到"义"的精准且唯一的定义,很多时候需要根据不同语境去"意会"。

以"greater good"翻译"义"也不是尽善尽美的译法，因为它隐含"牺牲少数利益"的暗示。参见英文词典对"the greater good"的释义：

The benefit or betterment of the majority of people, especially at the cost of smaller or individual concerns. (thefreedictionary.com)

《纽约时报》报道债务问题的一段文字，或可给上述词典释义做一个注解：

The government has virtually unlimited power to head off crises by directing resources – and apportioning pain – as it sees fit, often by ordering banks and other creditors to accept losses for the greater good before things get out of hand. (*The New York Times*, March 26, 2023)

"apportion pain（分摊痛苦）""accept losses（接受损失）"，以实现"greater good"。也许以同义词"common good"翻译"义利观"可弱化这方面暗示。

同理，当"道法自然"进入外交语境，当"大道至简"写入《政府工作报告》，译者不宜从词典上照搬一个"Tao"了事，而是需要让译文契合具体语境，让语言尽量简洁流畅，上下通达。

中华文明历来崇尚天人合一、道法自然，追求人与自然和谐共生。（习近平在"领导人气候峰会"上的讲话，2021-4-22）

The Chinese civilization has always valued harmony between man and Nature as well as observance of the laws of Nature. It has been our constant pursuit that man and Nature could live in harmony with each other.

大道至简，政简易行。（2023 年《政府工作报告》）

Great truths are always simple, and simple government administration is always most effective.

概念的意会性常常令密切观察中国的外媒摸不着头脑。《经济学人》曾撰文详解"国之大者"四个字，认为这四个字"无所不包（a catch-all）"，很抽象。正如《解放军报》评论文章"一定要牢记'国之大者'"（2022-11-29）所指出的：人民的幸福生活是"国之大者"，保护好生态环境也是"国之大者"；"两个大局"是"国之大者"，协调发展、协同发展、共同发展也是"国之大者"；为中国梦强军梦贡献力量是"国之大者"，为国分忧、为国解难、为国尽责也是"国之大者"。如何翻译"国之大者"才最贴切？是"the main affairs of state"还是"national priorities"，抑或是"the country's most fundamental interests"？似乎难有定论。

意会性还体现在句法层面。正如翻译理论家尤金·奈达（Eugene Nida）在 *Translating Meaning* 一书中指出的，中英文最显著的差异也许是形合（hypotaxis）与意合（parataxis）。

英文重形合（hypotaxis），起承转合离不开"but""and"等连接词；中文重意合（parataxis），逻辑关系比较隐晦。《毛泽东选集》英译专家程镇球先生指出，由于汉语属于分析性语言（analytical language），缺乏屈折变化（inflections），句子各部分的相互关系不是十分明显，需要从上下文和整句整段意思中去推敲，稍一不慎，就会出错。（《翻译论文集》）

党的二十大报告第 13 部分聚焦 "一国两制"，有这样一句关键表述：坚决打击反中乱港乱澳势力。

"反中" 与 "乱港乱澳" 的逻辑关系是什么？如果不假思索译为并列关系，试品一下译文：

We will crack down hard on those who are against China and attempt to create chaos in Hong Kong and Macao.

如此翻译给读者的感觉是：打击面过于宽泛。从用词上看，"are against" 与 "crack down hard" 轻重失衡，似乎凡是不赞成中国的，就要被坚决打击了。这既不符合中国立场，也不利于中国形象的塑造。

从上下文去推敲，不难发现，"乱港乱澳（则'反中'不言自明）" 是本句特别强调的重点，因此，"反中" 与 "乱港乱澳" 不宜译成并列关系，宜将 "乱港乱澳" 译成限定性定语从句。调整如下：

We will crack down hard on anti-China elements who attempt to create chaos in Hong Kong and Macao.

正如程镇球先生所言，局部要服从全局。对一个词来讲，全句是全局，一个段落是全局，整篇文章也是全局，必须加以考虑。

2023 年《政府工作报告》中有一长句，内含 11 个逗号，12 个平行短句：

（1）面对经济新的下行压力，（2）果断应对、及时调控，（3）动用近年储备的政策工具，（4）靠前实施既定政策举措，（5）坚定不移推进供给侧结构性改革，（6）出台实施稳经济一揽子政策和接续措施，（7）部署稳住经济大盘工作，（8）加强对地方落实政策的督导服务，（9）支持各地挖掘政策潜力，（10）支持经济大省勇挑大梁，（11）突出稳增长稳就业稳物价，（12）推动经济企稳回升。

第（6）句"出台实施稳经济一揽子政策"与第（7）句"部署稳住经济大盘工作"有明显的语义交叉，若并列译出，英文读起来重复感特别明显。面对12个平行小句，译者要花一番心思理顺其中逻辑关系，恰当分句甚至分段。

中文句子结构可以"一逗到底"，这是中文意合性的体现，但英文应尽量避免，否则就成了现代英文中普遍视为语病的"逗号粘连（comma splice）"。"逗号粘连"指的是，本该以冒号、分号或者连接词连接两个独立分句，却以逗号连接，使得句子间逻辑关系缺失。比如，"I love to read books, they are a great source of knowledge and entertainment."这句话中两个分句以逗号连接，逻辑关系模糊。可以把逗号改成分号或者句号，或者改为连词"because"，句子读来更加连贯清晰。

路透社翻译中国时政话语常常在句法形式上"照猫画虎"，出现"逗号粘连"。比如：

目前，疫情防控进入新阶段，仍是吃劲的时候，大家都在坚忍不拔努力，曙光就在前头。大家再加把劲，坚持就是胜利，团结就是胜利。

At present, the epidemic prevention and control is entering a new phase, it is still a time of struggle, everyone is persevering and working hard, and the dawn is ahead. Let's work harder, persistence means victory, and unity means victory. (Reuters, January 1, 2023)

中文只有两句话,第一句包含四个短句,第二句包含三个短句,都以逗号隔开,这种行文方式在中文写作中是可以接受的。路透社译文在形式上紧贴中文,一逗到底,使得英译文在清晰（clarity）与流畅连贯（flow）方面大打折扣。修改"逗号粘连"其实不难,可以把逗号改成分号或者句号,还可以增补连接词。路透社译法可以调整为:

At present, the epidemic prevention and control is entering a new phase. It is still a time of struggle, and everyone is persevering and working hard. The dawn is ahead. Let's work harder. Persistence means victory, and unity means victory.

在英文中,有时为了修辞需要,也会故意舍弃连接词（conjunction）构成意合句。最经典的,狄更斯《双城记》第一章以意合句开篇:

It was the best of times, it was the worst of times, it was the age of wisdom, it was the age of foolishness, it was the epoch of belief, it was the epoch of incredulity, it was the season of light, it was the season of darkness, it was the spring of hope, it was the winter of despair.

十个"it was"独立短句，九个逗号，五组对比（best/worst; wisdom/foolishness; belief/incredulity; light/darkness; hope/despair），高度概括了时代的矛盾与复杂，为小说奠定了基调。若加入"and"连接词，会破坏句子节奏与平衡，反倒显得画蛇添足了。

恺撒大帝有句名言："I came, I saw, I conquered."，若以"and"隔开"I saw"与"I conquered"，便割断了文气，霸气锐减。然而，英文中的意合句毕竟是少数，除非修辞需要，应谨慎使用。

非确指性

与概念和句法层面的"意会性"密切相关的是时政话语中用词的"非确指性"或"模糊性"。

非确指性表达使用频率高，表现形式多样，或含蓄收敛，或避实就虚，或委婉朦胧。非确指性表达既方便讲话者表明态度，同时留下回旋余地和阐释空间。请看：

> 抓好家庭农场和农民合作社发展，加快发展农业社会化服务
>
> (We) ensured solid development of family farms and farmers' cooperatives, and accelerated the development of commercial services for agriculture.
>
> 稳定粮食播种面积，抓好油料生产
>
> We should keep total grain acreage at a stable level, promote the production of oilseed crops...

<u>加大对企业稳岗扩岗支持力度</u>

(We) <u>stepped up</u> efforts to <u>support</u> enterprises in stabilizing and expanding employment.

<u>积极的财政政策要加力提效</u>

We should <u>enhance the intensity and effectiveness</u> of our proactive fiscal policy. (2023年《政府工作报告》)

"加大……力度""抓好……发展""进一步提高""着力推进""深入实施""做好""靠前"等一系列非确指性表达的共性是：抽象（abstract）、模糊（vague）。这与外媒写作力求用词"具体（specific）""实在（concrete）"形成鲜明对比。

面对避实就虚的表达，译者"辗转腾挪"的空间并不大。按照翻译标准，译者应"摹写其神情，仿佛其语气"，原文抽象模糊，译文自然也得抽象模糊。

党的二十大报告中有这样一句："督促领导干部特别是高级干部严于律己、严负其责、严管所辖"。

具体翻译中，译者面临一个问题：何为"严管所辖"？所辖的"对象"是"人（比如下属）"还是"事"？明确所辖对象，关乎译文句式和措辞的选择，因此译者必须刨根问底。经询，得到权威解释：所辖者，既包括人，也包括事。结合上下文，出于简洁考虑，译者只能在译文中保留原文的模糊性："conduct rigorous management within their jurisdictions"。

党的二十大报告中多次出现"斗争"二字。如何理解"斗争"，需要具体问题具体分析。比如，"反腐败斗争"指向比较明确，可以译成比较实的词"battle"："wage a battle against corruption on a scale unprecedented in our history（开展了史无前例的反腐败斗争）"。但有些"斗争"比较模糊，译得太实会造成严重误解。牛津大学中国中心主任郝拓德（Todd H. Hall）教授曾撰文指出，若是把"统筹加强各方向各领域军事斗争"里的"军事斗争"照字面直译成"military fighting"，会给英文读者"中国要与所有人打仗"的错误印象。实际上，"加强各方向各领域军事斗争"结合具体语境更恰当的解读是："努力克服困难、取得进步（striving to overcome obstacles and achieve progress）"。[1]

官方译本将此句中的"军事斗争"这一非确指性表述模糊处理成"military work"，避免了郝拓德所担心的错误印象，也是深刻领悟原文内涵的译法。

> 统筹加强各方向各领域军事斗争
>
> We have coordinated efforts to strengthen military work in all directions and domains...

译者要特别注意拿捏用词的分寸，当原文用词含蓄收敛，译文也不能"擅自加码"。比如：

> 我国外贸稳增长仍面临较大压力。（2023年上半年进出口情况新闻发布会）
>
> China still faces much pressure in ensuring steady rise in foreign trade.
>
> 基本实现国家治理体系和治理能力现代化（党的二十大报告）

---

[1] https://interpret.csis.org/dare-to-fight-or-dare-to-struggle-translation-of-a-chinese-political-concept/

basically modernize the system and capacity for governance

如果把"面临较大压力"译成"face great pressure",在语气上就拔高一度,把"great"改成"much"在语气上尽量贴近原文。党的二十大报告中多次提到"基本实现",英译文均要保留"basically/basic"这一修饰词。

非确指性还体现在"委婉语(euphemism)"的使用,比如"全域静态管理(whole-area static management)""按下'暂停键'(hit the pause button)""原则上(in principle)"等。"原则上"三个字很值得玩味,常常令听者猜不透。翻译委婉语,译者有时面临一个窘境:若照字面直译,可能文理不通,令人不知所云。若在译文中"捅破那层窗户纸",又失去了委婉语的功能。外交部常用"个别政客/国家"代指"某个政客/国家",而非指名道姓,保留一点外交的体面。英译时也只能"依样画葫芦"译成"certain politician/country"。笔者在工作实践中常常遇到关于职务翻译的难题,比如这段新闻发布会通告里的"负责人"三个字:

中共中央宣传部于 2022 年 8 月 24 日(星期三)上午举行"中国这十年"系列主题新闻发布会,请文化和旅游部副部长 XXX、艺术司负责人 XXX、公共服务司负责人 XXX、非物质文化遗产司司长 XXX、产业发展司司长 XXX 和国家文物局政策法规司司长 XXX 介绍推动新时代文化和旅游高质量发展有关情况,并答记者问。(国新网)

从常识来看,"某司负责人"应该指的是"某司一把手(the most senior official)"。但是,笔者检索后发现,"负责人"常常并非一把手，一把手反而另有其人。这就给翻译出了难题：若是把"负责人"译为"a person in charge of"或者"chief/head/director"，极易给人错觉，与现实情况不符。中文故意以"负责人"模糊表述，大概是为了与后面的一众"司长"尽量匹配。既然中文不愿点明真实官衔，那英译时也不妨模糊处理："a senior official of ..."。类似的，当遇到"某部领导成员"，译者也只能老老实实地译成"a leading member"；遇到"省部级主要领导干部"，也只能译成"principal officials at the provincial and ministerial level"。

非确指性表达并非中文时政话语的专利，欧美官方表态也常常避实就虚。比如，"we must take radical / all appropriate measures"。

英国前首相伊丽莎白·特拉斯（Liz Truss）在短短五分钟的胜选演讲中连讲数次"deliver"。请看其中五例：

... deliver on the energy crisis

应对好能源危机

We will deliver over the next two years.

未来两年，我们会干出成绩！

I know that we will deliver, we will deliver and we will deliver.

我相信，我们会干出成绩！我们会干出成绩！我们会干出成绩！

"deliver"的意思是"to produce the promised, desired, or expected results"（*Merriam Webster*）。从词典释义也能看出，这个词指向并不具体，常用于抽象朦胧的表态。

近年来，美国高级别官员频繁使用"pacing challenge"一词描述中国。请看：

> We've known that the PRC is the <u>pacing geopolitical challenge</u> of our era – one that will test American diplomacy like few issues in recent memory.
>
> 我们已经知道，中华人民共和国是我们这个时代的地缘政治步调挑战——一个在我们近期记忆中罕见的考验美国外交的挑战。（"美国驻华大使馆"公众号，2023-2-17）

早在 2021 年初，美国国防部长劳埃德·奥斯汀（Lloyd Austin）首次公开使用"pacing challenge"来描述中国。近年来，这一提法热度逐渐上升。外媒报道时都会补充一句解释，否则一般英文读者真不容易看懂。

英国《卫报》称这一表述"有些朦胧（slightly nebulous[1]）"，并这样解释其内涵：

> In recent weeks, the official catchphrase for Beijing has been the <u>slightly nebulous</u> "pacing challenge", <u>suggesting the US is the world's constant frontrunner with China ever closer to its shoulder.</u> (February 15, 2023)

美国福克斯新闻网（FOX NEWS）这样解读：

> ... which refers to <u>a competitor making significant</u>

---

[1] Nebulous: (especially of ideas) unclear and lacking form（《剑桥高级学习词典》）

progress toward challenging US defense strategy. (January 19, 2021)

《卫报》与福克斯新闻网对"pacing challenge"一词的解释似乎也并不完全一致，可见模糊性政治表达具备一定的阐释余地。我们回头看美国驻华大使馆公众号给出的官方译法："步调挑战"。显然，"步调挑战"是按英文字面直译，正如美国读者对"pacing challenge"感到陌生，中文读者见到"步调挑战"这四个字估计也是一脸问号。原文模糊，官方译者也不敢迈开步子，恐落人口实。这情有可原。

如果想让中文读者读懂"pacing challenge"这一重要提法，我们不妨结合外媒的解释，把这个词说得明白些。

在奥斯汀看来，中俄都对美国构成挑战，但发展势头正好相反。奥斯汀原话是：Russia is also a threat, but it is in decline. 对比来看，"a pacing challenge"其实就是"a formidable and ever-growing challenge（既不容小觑又与日俱增的挑战）"。美国官方也许还会延续"步调挑战"这一模糊译法，但我们要尽量搞清楚这一重要提法的内涵。

英国政治思想家以赛亚·伯林（Isaiah Berlin）这样评价政治话语的模糊性：

> Social and political terms are necessarily vague. The attempt to make the vocabulary of politics too precise may render it useless. But it is no service to the truth to loosen usage beyond necessity. (*Two Concepts of Liberty*)

社会和政治语言必然是模糊的。政治语言太精确可能流于无用，但若用词宽泛过了头，亦无益于追求真理。（《自由论》）

很多时候，立法和政治语言故意不精确，保留一定的模糊性。2023 年 7 月 1 日起施行的修订版《中华人民共和国反间谍法》将受保护的客体从"国家秘密、情报"扩大为"其他关系国家安全和利益的文件、数据、资料、物品"。修订版新增的模糊化表述属于概括式立法语言，扩大了相关主体窃密的对象范围。这一立法语言的变化受到外媒广泛关注。

同时，我们也应认识到，语言的模糊性要"张弛有度"，不可过头。政治话语的模糊性与国际传播的大众属性存在一定的矛盾。尤其需要注意的是，我们的政治话语里行话术语和非确指性表述较多，对外传播时不能"一翻了之"，要变通表达方式，或者如《卫报》等外媒那样做好阐释工作。

固定性

特别重视"提法（formulation）"，是中国时政话语或者说中国政治文化的一个重要特点。

在我们的政治文化下，一个提法的微调、弃用或者重提，往往传递政策调整的信号。比如，20 世纪 80 年代初，官方曾发文通知，不再提"劳动致富（achieving wealth through labor）"，改提"勤劳致富（achieving wealth through diligence）"。这两个提法在日常交流中并无明确界限，但在政治话语中，一字之差反映了思想的改变和政策的调整。"劳动"二字侧重体力劳动，在改革开放的大背景下，提法的微调意味着多元化致富途径受到认可与包容。时至今日，官方叙事基本上以"鼓励勤劳创新致富"替代"劳动致富"。

瑞典汉学家沈迈克注意到中国时政话语里"提法"的标志性特点：

> A defining characteristic of the formulation is its fixed form.
>
> 提法的一个显著特征是：形式固定。

比如，"一带一路"倡议这个提法里的"倡议（initiative）"二字不能随便变更。外国学者以及外媒有时把"一带一路"倡议描述成"战略（strategy）""计划（plan）"等，但中国官方表述不会如此随意。

提法的固定性深刻影响着英文翻译实践。提法离不开中国政治文化土壤。很多关键提法高度浓缩，应用场域极广，译者要在"固定性"与"灵活性"之间取得最佳平衡，既兼顾英文表达习惯，也要防止灵活过了头，窄化提法内涵。

以"党建"这一重要提法为例。在党的二十大报告中，"党的建设/党建"一词应用语境丰富多元。比如：

> 坚定不移全面从严治党，深入推进新时代党的建设新的伟大工程
>
> 抓党建促乡村振兴，加强城市社区党建工作，推进以党建引领基层治理
>
> 全面提高机关党建质量，推进事业单位党建工作

在报告英文版中，分别以"strengthen the Party"（2次）、"Party building"（14次）英译"党建"。单从英文表达角度看，"Party building"是"党建"二字的字面直译，的确不如"strengthen the Party"自然明了。但是，"党建"这一提法在中国时政话语中有多种多样的应用语境，明了易懂的"strengthen the Party"并非万能译法，比如：

> 加快形成覆盖党的领导和党的建设各方面的党内法规制度体系（《习近平谈治国理政》第三卷）
>
> We will act more quickly to put in place a system of Party rules and regulations that covers all aspects of Party leadership and Party development.

"党建"作为反复出现的符号性提法，英文表述似不宜做过多的变换，这既有用词简洁的考虑，也有政治提法固定性的考虑。若脱离语境，在"真空"状态下评价"Party building"是否地道，并无实际意义。在报告的完整语境下，读者也不会把"Party building"理解成"党的建筑物"。

从"党建"一词的英译可见，译者力求在提法的固定性与译文的可读性之间寻求中道。"变"与"不变"，是英译中国时政话语的一体两面。当变则变，是翻译这门艺术的内在要求；当不变则不变，也是译者深刻把握中国时政话语风格特点后的主动选择。这是翻译的辩证法。

有的英文读者把这类固定提法称之为"set phrase（定式表达）"或者更具负面色彩的"jargon（行话术语）"。"jargon"的频繁出现，一方面加重了文字的政治和意识形态色彩，另一方面也使文字晦涩难懂。

jargon: You use jargon to refer to words and expressions that are <u>used in special or technical ways by particular groups of people, often making the language difficult to understand</u>.
(《柯林斯高级英语学习词典》)

曾有读者留言提问：一定要把"推进中华民族伟大复兴"翻译成"advance national rejuvenation / advance the (great) rejuvenation of the Chinese nation"吗？可否翻译成更通俗易懂的"make China great again"？

CGTN主持人王冠在其专著《让世界听懂中国》一书中也对这一表述的译法提出思考："the (great) rejuvenation of the Chinese nation"虽然意思准确，但稍显书面语气。他认为在半官方或者非官方场合，可尝试用"短平快"的英文来表达"中华民族伟大复兴"。

类似的问题还有很多。比如有人提出："高举中国特色社会主义伟大旗帜"可否译成"短平快"的英文"uphold socialism with Chinese characteristics"？

笔者认为，上述问题的本质是：如何在改进对外表达"文风"上做一点尝试，即如何在中文政治提法的固定性与英文译文的可读性之间求平衡。

回答这些问题，没有绝对答案，还是要视应用场合和文本特点而定。翻译党的二十大报告、政府工作报告这类严肃的政治文本，译者应清楚提法的固定性在中国政治文化中的重要作用，译法的变换应以不歪解提法内涵、不影响整体文风、不引起外界误读为前提。这也是翻译的本质要求。然而，我们也应认识到，固定提法的频繁出现有时会影响英文读者的阅读体验，甚至"拒人于千里之外"。因而国际传播工作者需要在把握提法内涵的基础上，在上下文明确的前提下，善于把"固定译法"转换成通俗易懂的表达。

以"共同富裕"为例。党的二十大报告八次提到"共同富裕"，其中六次翻译成"common prosperity"，有两次调整为"(bring/promote) prosperity to/for all"：

> 着力维护和促进社会公平正义，着力促进<u>全体人民共同富裕</u>，坚决防止两极分化。
>
> We will endeavor to maintain and promote social fairness and justice, <u>bring prosperity to all</u>, and prevent polarization.

> 人的全面发展、<u>全体人民共同富裕</u>取得更为明显的实质性进展；
>
> ... make more notable and substantive progress in <u>promoting</u> the people's well-rounded development and <u>prosperity for all</u>.

2022年1月，全球最大对冲基金桥水基金创始人雷·戴利奥（Ray Dalio）积极评价"共同富裕"，引美国媒体纷纷报道。戴利奥原话是：

> Common prosperity is a good thing. <u>It's another way of saying prosperity for most people.</u>

第二句是对"共同富裕"这一概念的阐释（paraphrase），以便让英文听众更好地理解"common prosperity"。这句阐释很有必要，因为"common prosperity"这一搭配在英文中并不常见。用一位英国外专的话说：

"Common prosperity" is not a commonly used phrase in English. It's not something you hear in the English-speaking world.

《华尔街日报》报道时开篇一句这样写：

Ray Dalio backed China's push for "common prosperity," or greater equality. (January 10, 2022)

《华尔街日报》编辑部意识到一般英文读者对"common prosperity"一词会感到陌生，因此及时用西方老百姓熟悉的概念"greater equality"加以阐释，与戴利奥的"prosperity for most people"一样，目的都是方便读者理解，因为没有哪个国家的人民不渴望增进平等、缩减贫富差距。这两种阐释虽与"common prosperity"含义不完全一致，但体现了将中国特色表述进行全球化表达的一种受众意识。

以"共同富裕"为代表的诸多中国特色提法，常常面临"阐释力"不足的问题。国际传播工作者不能仅仅满足于"译出来"，还得学会"讲出去"。提法的"壳"固然不变，但它的内涵必然要与时代同频共振；当译法之外的阐释跟不上，或者阐释笨拙，会直接影响关键提法的对外传播效果。新加坡国立大学院士、新加坡前常驻联合国代表马凯硕（Kishore Mahbubani）在《中国的选择：中美博弈与战略抉择》（*Has China Won?*）一书中写道：中国在阐释、捍卫自身立场方面，历来表现笨拙。

在笔者看来，"表现笨拙"很大一部分原因就是"译力有余而阐释力不足"。从这个角度讲，翻译只是国际传播工作的基础工程，提高国际传播效能，只会翻译是远远不够的。把方块字转化成字母不难，难的是让中国声音传得更远。

"修辞"密布

修辞密布，是当前时政话语的一大特点。无论是讲话致辞，还是政策报告，抑或是理论时评，都会用到各种修辞手法，最常见的当属对偶、排比和隐喻。试看党的二十大报告中的对偶与排比句：

紧紧抓住人民最关心最直接最现实的利益问题，坚持<u>尽力而为、量力而行</u>，<u>深入群众、深入基层</u>，采取更多<u>惠民生、暖民心</u>举措。

To this end, we must <u>do everything within our capacity</u> to resolve the most practical problems that are of the greatest and most direct concern to the people. We will <u>stay engaged with our people and their communities</u>, adopt more measures that <u>deliver real benefits to the people and win their approval</u>.

许多领域实现<u>历史性变革、系统性重塑、整体性重构</u>。

This enabled us to achieve <u>historic, systemic, and holistic</u> transformations in many fields.

<u>实现好、维护好、发展好</u>最广大人民根本利益。

We must strive to <u>realize, safeguard, and advance</u> the fundamental interests of all our people.

<u>尊重自然、顺应自然、保护自然</u>，是全面建设社会主义现代化国家的内在要求。

Respecting, adapting to, and protecting nature is essential for building China into a modern socialist country in all respects.

全党同志务必不忘初心、牢记使命，务必谦虚谨慎、艰苦奋斗，务必敢于斗争、善于斗争。

It is imperative that all of us in the Party never forget our original aspiration and founding mission, that we always stay modest, prudent, and hard-working, and that we have the courage and ability to carry on our fight.

隐喻修辞在中国时政话语中有多种表现形式，常见的有"军事隐喻（military metaphor）""动物隐喻（animal metaphor）""天气隐喻（weather metaphor）""疾病隐喻（illness metaphor）""道路隐喻（road metaphor）""船舶隐喻（ship metaphor）""舞台隐喻（stage metaphor）""旗帜隐喻（flag metaphor）"等。试举几例：

集中力量实施脱贫攻坚战。（军事隐喻）

We have pooled resources to wage a critical battle against poverty.（党的二十大报告）

反腐败斗争就一刻不能停，必须永远吹冲锋号。（军事隐喻）

We must keep sounding the bugle and never rest, not even for a minute, in our fight against corruption.（党的二十大报告）

腐败是危害党的生命力和战斗力的最大毒瘤。（疾病隐喻）

Corruption is a <u>cancer</u> to the vitality and ability of the Party.（党的二十大报告）

以猛药去疴、重典治乱的决心，以刮骨疗毒、壮士断腕的勇气，坚持反腐败无禁区、全覆盖、零容忍。（疾病隐喻）

<u>Just as heavy doses of medicine are needed to treat serious disease, stringent measures must be applied to address serious corruption.</u> To this end, the Party has allowed no safe haven, left no ground unturned, and shown no tolerance in fighting corruption.（《中国共产党的历史使命与行动价值》）

不敢腐、不能腐、不想腐一体推进，<u>"打虎""拍蝇""猎狐"</u>多管齐下。（动物隐喻）

We have taken coordinated steps to see that officials do not have the audacity, opportunity, or desire to be corrupt, and we have used a combination of measures to <u>"take out tigers," "swat flies," and "hunt down foxes,"</u> punishing corrupt officials of all types.（党的二十大报告）

坚决惩治群众身边的<u>"蝇贪"</u>。（动物隐喻）

Firm action will be taken to swat <u>"flies," or corrupt low-ranking officials</u>, whose misconduct directly affects people's lives.（党的二十大报告）

中国特色强军之<u>路</u>越走越<u>宽广</u>。（道路隐喻）

The Chinese <u>path</u> to building a strong military is growing ever <u>broader</u>.（党的二十大报告）

推动我国迈上全面建设社会主义现代化国家新征程。（道路隐喻）

We have ... taken China on a new journey toward building a modern socialist country in all respects.（党的二十大报告）

国家无论大小、强弱、贫富，都应该做和平的维护者和促进者，不能这边搭台、那边拆台，而应该相互补台、好戏连台。（舞台隐喻）

Countries, whether big or small, strong or weak, rich or poor, should all contribute their share to maintaining and enhancing peace. Rather than undercutting each other's efforts, countries should complement each other and work for joint progress.（习近平在博鳌亚洲论坛2013年会上的主旨演讲）

引领和保障中国特色社会主义巍巍巨轮乘风破浪、行稳致远。（船喻+天气隐喻）

Under its guidance, we will ensure that the great ship of socialism with Chinese characteristics catches the wind, cuts through the waves, and sails steadily into the future.（党的二十大报告）

回归祖国后，香港战胜各种风雨挑战，稳步前行。（天气隐喻）

Since its return, Hong Kong has overcome various *hardships* and challenges and advanced steadily forward.（习近平在庆祝香港回归祖国25周年大会暨香港特别行政区第六届政府就职典礼上的讲话）

高举中国特色社会主义伟大旗帜（旗帜隐喻）

hold high the great banner of socialism with Chinese characteristics（党的二十大报告）

围绕举旗帜、聚民心、育新人、兴文化、展形象建设社会主义文化强国。（旗帜隐喻）

In our efforts to turn China into a country with a thriving socialist culture, we will focus on upholding socialism with Chinese characteristics, rallying public support, fostering a new generation of young people, developing Chinese culture, and better presenting China to the world.（党的二十大报告）

"red flag（红旗）"在英文中具有鲜明的意识形态色彩。《剑桥高级学习词典》对"red flag"有专门释义："a flag used as a symbol of revolution"。《经济学人》也曾以"展红旗（unfurl red flags）"来表达"展露/宣扬社会主义立场"。请看：

> Second, that it is not a bunch of closet Corbynites[1], touting pro-business policies before the election and unfurling red flags after it. (*The Economist*, April 27, 2023)

英文也习惯以天气喻政治时局。在美国大选语境下，外媒写作常用"storm clouds loom for Democrats/Republicans"这种隐喻表达，"storm cloud"是暴风雨来临时的滚滚黑云，"黑云压城"必然不是什么好兆头。《经济学人》报道中美关系，也以暴风雨

---

[1] 工党前党魁杰里米·科尔宾（Jeremy Corbyn）自称"社会主义者"。"closet Corbynites（潜伏的科尔宾分子）"指的是在意识形态上与科尔宾暗合之人。

作喻：

During Donald Trump's four years in the White House, tempests buffeted relations between America and China.

"tempest" 意思是 "a violent storm"，"buffet" 意思是 "to hit heavily and repeatedly"。鉴于中英文在天气隐喻上的共同点，直译便常常成为首选之道。比如：

我们必须增强忧患意识，坚持底线思维，做到居安思危、未雨绸缪，准备经受风高浪急甚至惊涛骇浪的重大考验。（党的二十大报告）

We must therefore be more mindful of potential dangers, be prepared to deal with worst-case scenarios, and be ready to withstand high winds, choppy waters, and even dangerous storms.

很多时候，隐喻、夸张、排比多种修辞手法同时使用。比如：

"海水不干，打私不断"。走私一直是国际贸易的毒瘤，危害国家安全和经济秩序，有的还影响人民生命健康。（"守国门、促发展，为推进中国式现代化贡献海关力量"新闻发布会，2023-3-20）

这句话既有隐喻（走私是……毒瘤），又有夸张（海水不干）。

善用修辞手法，可以体现写作者的文采与想象力。作为中国时政话语的一大叙事特点，修辞密布给文章增色，但同时给英译工作者带来巨大挑战。

中文的排比句直译成英文，极易给人"冗余（redundancy）"之感。比如：

自我净化、自我完善、自我革新、自我提高能力显著增强。（党的二十大报告）

We have significantly boosted the Party's ability to purify, improve, renew, and excel itself.

四个英文动词"purify""improve""renew""excel"有明显的语义交叉，英文读来略带冗余感。但是，作为中国时政话语里的固定提法，"四个自我"内容各有侧重，并非仅仅是一种修辞形式，因此译者不便随意删减，只能尽可能根据其语义的重点，推敲选用准确、地道的词来表达。

琼·平卡姆（Joan Pinkham）在《中式英语之鉴》一书中无奈地指出，不光是中国译者，英文母语者也容易用词冗余。英国《经济学人》曾专门撰文反思冗余的利弊，指出，现实中不可能杜绝冗余，冗余有其用武之地。（"'Omit needless words!' But not all of them", March 16, 2023）

古今中外，让文字简单明了都是高水平写作者追求的文风。法国哲学家、数学家布莱兹·帕斯卡（Blaise Pascal）曾抱歉地写道"我实在没有时间把信写得短一些"。看来，把文字写得冗长不是难事，难的是言简意赅。翻译是戴着镣铐跳舞，不似写作那般自由，译者要时刻受到原文的羁绊，而英译政治内涵复杂微妙的时政话语，就更无多少"自由裁量权"了。

其他修辞，如隐喻、夸张、用典，都是英译时政话语中的难点，译者对其可谓"又爱又恨"。爱其表达生动形象，恨其难译，稍有不慎便迷失在翻译中。此中苦乐，且待后文分解。

"缩略语"云集

缩略语云集，是中国时政话语的一大显著特点。缩略语具有言简义丰、易于传播、方便记忆等特点，在各级政府公文写作中应用频率很高。2023年《政府工作报告》中有多处缩略语，笔者归纳如下：

"两个确立""四个意识""四个自信""两个维护"；

"两不愁三保障""三区三州""四个不摘""六稳""六保"；

"双随机、一公开"，"两个毫不动摇"，"三保"工作；

"一带一路"，"一国两制"，纠治"四风"，"三公"经费，"双拥"活动；

"证照分离""放管结合""港人治港""澳人治澳""爱国者治港""爱国者治澳"；

管中窥豹，可知数字缩略语在中国时政话语中比例较高。《经济学人》把"两个百年""四个全面"等数字缩略语称之为"numbered lists"，并指出数字缩略语在中国时政话语中"备受青睐"这一特点（China loves political slogans expressed as numbered lists.）。

时政话语中的缩略语也是一种"限定型语码"，对使用者与听者之间的话语共识和认知交集要求比较高。少数缩略语的大众普及率较高，比如"港人治港""四个自信""一国两制"等，而大量的缩略语受众较窄，需要一定的话语共识才能理解，比如"四不两直""七下八上"防汛期、"四不一无意"等。

英文中也有不少缩略语。比如，联合国提出的"Millennium Development Goals（千年发展目标）"；解决以色列—巴勒斯坦冲突的政治方案"The Two-State Solution（两国方案）"；由英美加澳新五个英语国家组成的情报组织"The Five Eyes（五眼联盟）"；特朗普的竞选口号"Make America Great Again（简称MAGA）"。

美国前总统罗斯福曾提出著名的"Four Freedoms（四大自由）"：the freedom of speech, the freedom of worship, the freedom from want, and the freedom from fear。

> Mr DeSantis and the Florida legislature ... will focus instead in the coming year on "three E's" – education, the economy and the environment – which are winning issues with voters. (*The Economist,* November 10, 2022)
>
> Germany's central bank chief Joachim Nagel listed deglobalisation as one of the "three Ds" that would "add to inflationary pressures" alongside decarbonisation and demographics. (*Financial Times*, May 23, 2022)
>
> Beijing's top court has said a "996" overtime policy, under which employees work 9 am to 9 pm, six days a week, is illegal. (*Financial Times*, August 7, 2021)
>
> Expert Comment: Five new(s) and five olds in the sixth IPCC report on mitigating climate change (Oxford University, April 26, 2022)

缩略语作为一种归纳性、概括性表达方式，在各种文化和语言中都有广阔的应用场景。

缩略语虽然好用，但翻译起来却是个麻烦事。英译非数字缩略语，关键是把缩略语指代的内容读懂读透，然后用清晰简洁的文字表达出来。比如：

坚持放管结合。（2023年《政府工作报告》）

While delegating power, we also improved regulation.

深入开展"双拥"活动。（同上）

... conduct extensive activities to promote mutual support between civilian sectors and the military.

改革商事制度，推行"证照分离"改革。（同上）

We carried out institutional reforms in the business sector and introduced the reform to separate out the business license from certificates required for starting a business.

英译数字缩略语，需要根据具体语境考虑是否在译文中保留数字结构。大体有两种情况。

第一，不拘泥于数字结构，"重意不重形"。

在2023年《政府工作报告》中，"四个意识""四个自信"分别只出现一次，可直接译出缩略语内涵，不必保留数字结构。比如：

增强"四个意识"、坚定"四个自信"

... enhanced their consciousness of the need to maintain political integrity, think in big-picture terms, follow the leadership core, and keep in alignment with the central Party leadership; <u>stayed confident in</u> the path, theory, system, and culture of socialism with Chinese characteristics...

很多数字缩略语具有鲜明的中国话语特色，在英文中还原其结构比较困难，这种情况下应"重意不重形"。比如：

坚持德才兼备、以德为先、<u>五湖四海</u>、任人唯贤，把新时代好干部标准落到实处。（党的二十大报告）

We must select officials on the basis of both integrity and ability, with greater weight given to integrity, and on the basis of merit <u>regardless of background</u>, thus fully applying the criteria for judging competent officials in the new era.

当前我国已进入"七下八上"防汛关键期。（党的二十大报告）

China enters the critical period of flood season <u>in the latter/second half of July and first half of August</u>.

第二，保留数字结构，并补充说明。党的二十大报告中提到"三个区分开来""四个全面"以及"五位一体"，英译文在正文中保留数字结构，并加注解释其内涵。如果在正文中详述其内涵，不仅冗长累赘，而且不利于上下文衔接。请看：

明确"五位一体"总体布局和"四个全面"战略布局，确定稳中求进工作总基调。

We have adopted <u>the Five-Sphere Integrated Plan and the</u>

Four-Pronged Comprehensive Strategy[1] as well as the general principle of pursuing progress while ensuring stability.

落实"三个区分开来",激励干部敢于担当、积极作为。

We should apply the "three distinctions,"[2] so as to encourage officials to boldly take on responsibilities and demonstrate enterprise in their work.

外媒在处理中国时政话语里的数字缩略语时,习惯保留数字结构,并以括号、连接词(比如"that is""i.e.")引出缩略语所指具体内容。或者另起一句,对缩略语作出解释。比如,外媒提到"四个自信""两个确立""四个全面"等缩略语时,这样表述:

Chinese must display "four self-confidences". Three of them are about strengthening belief in various aspects of Chinese communism. But the fourth relates to Chinese culture. (*The Economist,* April 27, 2023)

... embedded in the resolution: "The two establishments"

---

1 The Five-Sphere Integrated Plan is to promote coordinated economic, political, cultural, social, and ecological advancement. The Four-Pronged Comprehensive Strategy is to make comprehensive moves to build a modern socialist country, deepen reform, advance law-based governance, and strengthen Party self-governance.

2 The three distinctions refer to those between errors caused by lack of experience in pilot reforms and deliberate violations of discipline and law; between errors made in conducting experiments that are not explicitly restricted by higher-level authorities and arbitrary violations of discipline and law in the face of higher-level authorities' explicit prohibition; and between unwitting errors made in pursuing development and violations of discipline and law for personal gains.

("Liang ge queli") – that is, establishing... (*The New York Times*, November 16, 2021)

The "Four Comprehensives" refer to China working "comprehensively" to build a moderately prosperous society and strengthen reforms, rule of law and party discipline. (Reuters, February 26, 2015)

外媒普遍采用"直译＋阐释"或者"直译＋拼音＋阐释"的处理模式，有其内在逻辑：写作比翻译享有较高的自由度和灵活度，在文章中保留缩略语数字结构，辅以必要的阐释，在上下文语境的加持下不会影响读者理解，且有助于行文流畅。"数字＋"的构词形式可以灵活一点，不必拘泥于语法规范，与数字搭配的词可以是名词、动词、形容词甚至是字母。像"Four Comprehensives""Three Represents""Three E's""Four-sphere Confidence"这类创造性构词搭配，由于不太符合英文表达规范，外媒一般还会加上引号。可以说，通过保留数字结构，外媒在一定程度上让英文读者感受到了中国时政话语里缩略语的构词特点。

外媒的做法具有一定的参考价值。在对外报道实践中，不必每次遇到数字缩略语就去官方文件中"搬运"冗长的译文，不妨多一些灵活变通，遵循新闻写作规律，用自然流畅的表达把缩略语这一语言符号的所指讲清楚。在对外翻译实践中，在篇幅允许的情况下，也可在英文中保留数字结构并以括注等形式补充说明，使译文尽量明快。比如：

中方严正敦促美方……以实际行动恪守一个中国原则和中美三个联合公报规定，切实将美国领导人作出的

"四不一无意"承诺落到实处，不要在错误和危险的道路上越走越远。（外交部，2022-8-2）

It must take credible actions to observe strictly the one-China principle and the provisions of the three China-U.S. joint communiqués, deliver on the "five noes" commitment made by the U.S. leadership (i.e. not seek a "new Cold War"; not seek to change China's system; the revitalization of its alliances is not against China; not support "Taiwan independence"; not look for conflict with China), and not go further down the wrong and dangerous path.

数字缩略语的密集出现，势必降低文字的可读性。当缩略语沉淀为行话术语，其受众范围必然窄化。请看以下两例：

十九大、十九届六中全会提出的"十个明确""十四个坚持""十三个方面成就"概括了这一思想的主要内容，必须长期坚持并不断丰富发展。（党的二十大报告）

The main elements of this theory are summarized in the 10 affirmations, the 14 commitments, and the 13 areas of achievement that were articulated at the 19th National Congress and the Sixth Plenary Session of the 19th Party Central Committee, all of which we must adhere to over the long term and continue to enrich and develop.

习近平主席提出了"四个必须"，清晰阐明了中方在乌克兰问题上的权威主张。中方先后提出五点立场和缓解人道主义危机的六点倡议，为化解危机、缓和局势发出了中国声音、贡献了中国智慧。中国的作用主要体现

为五个坚持。（外交部，2022-4-1）

President Xi Jinping put forward the "four musts" and clearly stated China's authoritative position on the Ukraine issue. China has put forward a five-point position and a six-point initiative on easing the humanitarian crisis, making China's voice for and contributing China's wisdom to resolving the crisis and easing tensions. China's role is mainly reflected in five-pronged perseverance.

实践中，我们应结合任务特点以及缩略语出现的具体语境，灵活选择处理方法，不可拘泥于一端。同一缩略语在不同语境下，完全可以有不同的处理方式。

缩略语在中国时政话语中高频出现，其对内属性较强，本质上是一种"口号化的语言（sloganized language）"，是中文叙事方式的重要组成部分。未来，各种形式的缩略语仍会层出不穷，有些缩略语也许会逐渐被遗忘甚至被取代。

在面向大众的国际传播实践中，口号化的语言和行话术语不宜用得太频繁，这既是顾及英文叙事方式的需要，也是提高传播效能的需要。

2.1.2 外媒视角

曾有读者留言提问：为什么要把政府工作报告翻译成英文呢？难道仅仅是为了方便英文专业的学生学习翻译之用吗？

回答这个问题，需要有国家站位和国家视角。首先，在国家层面，英译党的二十大报告、政府工作报告，面向的受众不是国内的翻译爱好者或者英文专业学生，而是国外的政府、智库、媒体、企业、国际组织等。随着中国日渐走近世界舞台中央，外部观察解读中国的广度和深度都在加大，很多机构已不满足于从媒体报道的只言片语中窥视中国，而是希望更全面更系统地认识中国。

其次，英译国家级政治报告，是提高国际话语权的关键一环。2022年2月，美国著名智库"战略与国际研究中心（CSIS）"上线"解读：中国（Interpret: China）"翻译项目，全文翻译中国领导人讲话、重磅理论文章、重要政策文件等；2022年11月，美国非营利研究机构"战略翻译中心"正式上线，通过精细翻译并深入分析领导人讲话、重磅文章等，旨在读懂中国时政话语的字里行间。党的二十大报告、政府工作报告等顶层设计文件，内含国家治理的重要概念提法和关键政策表述，翻译国家队不能缺席，否则无异于把话语定义权和阐释权拱手让出。

中国重要的提法不但要主动对外译介，还要译好，不能草率。"一带一路"倡议最早被外媒译为"One Belt, One Road"，《经济学人》多次嘲笑该译文滑稽。

> To Western ears, "One Belt, One Road", as it was originally called, sounded inflexible: a China-centric view of how the world's infrastructure should be built. (*The Economist*, June 9, 2022)

对英文读者而言，"One Belt, One Road"听上去有些生硬，两个"One"在名称上给人"排他"感，即《经济学人》所谓的"中国中心"视角。2015年，为了弱化英译名引起的错误联想，"一带一路"倡议官方译法改为"The Belt and Road Initiative"，简写为

"BRI"。

鉴于中国时政话语的叙事特点，英译文在句法、词语、风格、修辞等方面自由发挥的空间并不大，这是由翻译的本质所决定的。可以预见，严肃的时政报告英译本读起来必然不会太美。《经济学人》曾对2023年《政府工作报告》英文版的文风做出如下评价：

> Like previous editions, the document is a combination of <u>theological boilerplate</u> ("hold high the great banner of socialism with Chinese characteristics"), <u>policy bromides</u> ("we should enhance the intensity and effectiveness of our proactive fiscal policy") and <u>technocratic factoids</u> (China increased the length of expressways by 30% and drainage pipelines by more than 40% over the past five years). (*The Economist*, March 10, 2023)

《经济学人》用三组关键词概括——"boilerplate""bromides""factoids"，且三个词都带有贬义，可见《经济学人》编辑部阅读报告英文版的体验并不愉快。先来看权威词典释义：

> boilerplate: formulaic or stereotypical language（《美国传统词典》）
>
> bromide: a commonplace remark or notion; a platitude（《美国传统词典》）
>
> factoids: invented facts, or facts that are real but trivial. (*Merriam Webster*)

比如，"Our thoughts and prayers are with those affected." 就是一句英文套语（boilerplate），每逢枪击案、自然灾害等天灾人祸，欧

美政客基本上都会讲这句话。权威英文词典告诉我们，"factoids"不等于"facts"，暗含"片面、断章取义"的负面意思。"factoid"一词由美国作家诺曼·梅勒（Norman Mailer）所创，在"fact"后面加上"-oid"，意在暗示与事实"相似但不相同（similar but not the same）"。《经济学人》曾这样描述"factoid"："roughly fact-shaped object that is not, in fact, a fact."（看上去像事实但实际上不是事实的东西）。"bromide"指的是"溴化物"，可用作镇静剂，引申开来表示"乏味无趣的套语"。好比"多喝热水"，虽然在表达关怀，但常被调侃直男不懂关怀。《经济学人》用词刁钻犀利可见一斑。

为了方便读者理解"policy bromides"一词，并加深对中英文时政话语非确指性的认识，笔者请生成式人工智能 Bing GPT 来举例说明。

问：Could you give me an example of a policy bromide?

Bing GPT: An example of a policy bromide might be <u>a politician saying "we need to create more jobs" without providing any specific or original ideas on how to achieve that goal</u>. This statement is intended to soothe or placate the public by addressing a common concern, but <u>it lacks originality or effectiveness because it does not provide any new or actionable information</u>.

实际上，美国媒体评价美国官方表态时也经常用"vague""empty"等词修饰"bromide"，又可见非确指性表达是中英文时政话语的一个共同点。2021年9月21日，美国总统拜登在第76届联合国大会上发表演讲，美国网络媒体 The New York Sun 毫不客气地指出：

In the whole history of the United Nations it's hard to think of a speech brimming with <u>emptier bromides</u> than President Biden's today at the General Assembly. "<u>Let's get to work</u>," is how he ended it. (September 21, 2021)

除了"Let's get to work",拜登演讲中充斥着大量的"policy bromides",比如:

To <u>deliver</u> for our own people, we must also <u>engage deeply</u> with the rest of the world.

To ensure that our own future, we must <u>work together</u> with other partners – our partners – <u>toward a shared future</u>.

And so, I believe we must <u>work together as never before</u>.

Let's <u>make our better future</u> now.

<u>We can do this</u>. It's within our power and capacity.

《经济学人》这三组关键词恰恰侧面印证了时政话语的风格特点。提法的"固定性",如"高举中国特色社会主义伟大旗帜""中华民族伟大复兴"等,决定了报告中必然不乏定式表述的重复。表达的非确指性,如"抓好""发挥好""积极的财政政策要加力提效"等,决定了报告中必然不乏抽象的政策表达。

笔者参与报告英文翻译工作,对外媒的评价其实并不感到意外。一方面,这是中国时政话语叙事特点决定的。政治文本不同于小说、散文、新闻等文体,不以文字"生动活泼"为第一要义。另一方面,外媒写作用词重具体忌抽象,风格恰恰与时政话语相反。在这种反差之下,《经济学人》读报告英文版感到乏味也在意料之中。毕竟,翻译政府工作报告,忠实原文并准确达意才是第一要义。

然而,《经济学人》的评论给我们一点启示:从国际传播视角,可在全译本之外准备节译本,择取报告要点、亮点,用更贴近英文读者的表达方式"编译"而非"翻译"。如此,文字或许可以走得更远。

2.1.3 汉学家视角

国际传播离不开翻译,这一点毋庸置疑。翻译是国际传播的基础工程,基础不牢地动山摇。但是,我们还要警惕一种错误认知:把国际传播等同于"翻译+传播"。这种有意无意的简单化认知,对有效开展国际传播造成巨大障碍。

翻译有翻译的标准和原则,传播有传播的内在规律。有时候,准确无误的翻译反而给传播,尤其是跨文化传播,帮倒忙。症结不在翻译质量的好与坏,而在中英文叙事方式的差异。

英文"narrative"既可以表示"story(故事)",也可以表示"the art of narrating(叙事方式)"。全世界的人都爱听故事,但是,不同的文化背景孕育了不同的叙事方式。英国汉学家、前外交官克里·布朗(Kerry Brown)指出(《海牙外交学研究》),欧美叙事方式喜欢营造高潮,且故事线清晰,中国的叙事方式常常与之不同。读过中国经典小说(比如《红楼梦》)的都知道,中国故事的讲述方式曲折复杂,常常令人难以把握。

哈佛大学肯尼迪学院教授、中国问题专家安东尼·赛奇进一步指出:"中文的叙事方式在中国很受欢迎,但在说英语的地方就不那么受欢迎了。"[1]

---

1 https://www.thepaper.cn/newsDetail_forward_12533093

叙事差异深刻影响着对外表达的"效能",必须加以重视。具体而言,有些表达在国内受欢迎,但在国际舆论场未必受欢迎。美国政治学者、普林斯顿大学教授范亚伦(Aaron Friedberg)在其著作 Getting China Wrong 一书中谈到外交语境下常讲的一句俗语:

朋友来了有好酒,敌人来了有猎枪。

We treat our friends with fine wine, but for our enemies we have shotguns.

这句话讲给国人听,十分提气,表达了捍卫国家利益的决心。然而,"好酒/猎枪论"在国际舆论场很容易被贴上"aggressive(好斗)""hostile(怀有敌意)"等标签。在范亚伦这位美国政治学者看来,"好酒/猎枪论"所流露出的"非友即敌"的二元对立,反映了一种"gangland mentality"。范亚伦的看法在西方社会很有代表性,背后的思维逻辑也不难理解。在现代国际关系中,国与国之间不宜简单地划分为朋友与敌人。从国际关系的历史与现实来看,非友非敌、似友似敌、忽友忽敌、可友可敌似乎比"非友即敌"更具有现实意义。

我们不应小觑叙事武断的危害性。美国迪堡大学传播学院教授吕行(Lucy Xing Lu)认为,话语的简单化会对认知与思辨造成负面影响。

As language was simplified, cognitive complexity was reduced, and the ability to think critically was deprived.

随着语言的简化,认知复杂度会降低,思辨能力会丧失。

叙事的简化与武断，容易孕育二元对立与极端思维。甜言蜜语者，舆论会轻易捧之为友，一起摩擦便骂之为敌。久而久之，人们容易丧失对地缘政治复杂性的认知。果真这般黑白分明，外交的门槛似乎就低了许多，备好美酒与猎枪，人人皆可成外交官。如此岂非儿戏？

重视叙事方式差异，认识到中文叙事方式在说英语的地方不一定受欢迎，进而认识到翻译在国际传播工作中有局限性，才有可能跳出翻译羁绊，创新对外表达。有外国读者指出，"与会专家一致认为（all those in attendance agreed）"这样的表达出现在英文新闻稿里令人反感，因为这样的叙事方式给英文读者这样的感觉：It just sounds like *propaganda*. 类似的例子还有很多。不是翻译得不够准确，而是通过准确无误的翻译把中文叙事方式"生搬"进英文，容易引起受众质疑甚至反感。

国际传播工作者时常要在翻译、编译、写作三种任务之间切换，因为仅靠翻译无法打通国际传播的"最后一公里"，甚至可能制造新问题。牛津大学历史学教授、汉学家沈艾娣（Henrietta Harrison）在其著作《翻译的危险：清朝与大英帝国两位翻译家的非凡人生》(*The Perils of Interpreting: The Extraordinary Lives of Two Translators Between Qing China and the British Empire*) 一书中谈到英国使团中两位译者的不同风格。一位是小斯当东（George Thomas Staunton），一位是传教士马礼逊（Robert Morrison）。

小斯当东从小开始学习中文，语言习得方式是与中国商人、水手交流对话，实践性和沟通性比较强。他的翻译风格是：淡化文化分歧，突出中英文化共性。马礼逊成年后才开始学习中文，最终目标是翻译《圣经》。马礼逊认为，翻译《圣经》不容"阐释（paraphrase）"。为了译好《圣经》，他着手编纂了第一部英汉字典。他的翻译风格是：一丝不苟，字字推敲，深入中国典籍中探求每个字的本义。

毫无疑问，论中文造诣，马礼逊技高一筹。然而，沈艾娣教授指出，马礼逊的翻译风格把中英文化差异放大了。对英文受众而言，他的精准直译（precise and literal translation）让中文显得异样又陌生。

沈艾娣透过晚清中英交流中的磕磕绊绊反观一百多年后的当下，并提醒读者：在 21 世纪的今天，把有中国特色的马克思主义"定式表达（set phrases）"直译到英文，几乎同样会令英文读者迷惑不解。

今天我们反复讲"中国特色"，中文叙事必然也离不开中国特色，而中国特色的关键就在于"两个结合"：把马克思主义基本原理同中国具体实际相结合、同中华优秀传统文化相结合。"第二个结合"在今后一段时期可能愈发重要。早在 2020 年，新加坡学者马凯硕在其著作《中国的选择》一书中就提醒西方民众，不要因为"communist"这一标签就轻视"中华文明（Chinese Civilization）"在推动中国发展进程中的重要地位。

用一种语言表达另一种文化里的概念，从来都不是容易事。用英文表达中国特色概念，尤其是中国传统文化概念，难度可想而知。今天的国际传播工作者似乎面临一个抉择：在对外讲好中国故事的实践中，应该效仿小斯当东还是马礼逊？

答案似乎是：二者都需要，都有用武之地。

加拿大汉学家贝淡宁（Daniel A. Bell）在《中国日报》撰文指出，把儒家概念"和"翻译成"harmony"一个词，给英文读者"整齐划一（sameness/uniformity/conformity）"的错觉，而儒家智慧里的"和"是尊重多元的。贝淡宁建议，"和"一字更好的译法是三个单词"diversity in harmony"。(*China Daily*, March 21, 2023)

西方文化尤其重视"多元性（diversity）"，在"和"字的英译文中点出"多元性"，更容易拉近与英文读者的距离。对外表达中国特色概念，我们要有跨文化视野，要多站在一般英文读者的视角去思考，从差异中寻找共同价值，拉近彼此距离。

今天的国际传播工作者不仅仅需要马礼逊式的"翻译力（translation）"，更需要小斯当东式的"阐释力（paraphrase）"。实际上，我们用中国叙事讲述英文故事反而更成功。比如，把"Coca-Cola"创造性地译成脍炙人口的"可口可乐"；把护肤品牌"La Mer"翻译成"海蓝之谜"。早期的共产党人把"The House of Communism"译成"亢慕义斋"，而非"共产主义之室"。"慕义"，多么有情怀、多么有中国韵味的译名啊！可见，早期的共产党人就有把马克思主义与中华优秀传统文化相结合的意识，也懂得如何让译文在目标受众中走得更远。反过来，我们难道不应该学会用英文的叙事方式创造性地讲好中国故事吗？

2.2 翻译中的误解与误用

经济学家金刻羽在其新书《新中国策略：超越社会主义和资本主义》(*The New China Playbook: Beyond Socialism and Capitalism*) 开篇写道：

> This book is about reading China in the original, coming to understand its people, economy, and government in such a way that the truth is not lost in translation, as is far too often the case.
>
> 本书旨在品读原汁原味的中国，希望以这样一种方式读懂中国人、中国经济、中国之治：确保中国的真实面貌不在翻译中迷失。在翻译中的误解与误用太常见了。

澳大利亚前总理陆克文（Kevin M. Rudd）也曾谈到"翻译的迷失"给国与国沟通造成障碍：很多中国人通过中译文了解美国，但是，译文常常在"准确性（accuracy）、细腻或者微妙之处（subtlety, or nuance）"不尽如人意。

略举一例。2020年10月3日，民主党总统候选人拜登发布一条推文：

> I'm running as a Democrat, but I will be an American president. Whether you voted for me or against me, I will represent you.

此推文一出，很多中文媒体这样报道：

拜登发推：我将成为美国总统。

拜登发布这条推文的前一天，时任总统特朗普感染新冠病毒。国内网民读此新闻，纷纷嘲笑拜登"太自信"："拜登应该是得到什么信儿了？""这么肯定能击败特朗普？"

中文媒体的译文让不懂英文的读者以为拜登在发表豪言壮语或者在幸灾乐祸，但实际上，拜登这条推文是在呼吁美国人团结。注意推文中的转折词"but"以及"American president"前面的不定冠词"an"。推文第一句的意思是："虽然我以民主党人身份竞选，但我要做全体美国人的总统。"形容词"American"指的是"全体美国人"，与前面的"a Democrat"相对。如果译成"虽然我以民主党人身份竞选，但是我将成为美国总统"，"虽然……但是"前后的逻辑转折是不通的。第二句进一步呼应第一句，告诉选民：无论你投票支持的是共和党还是民主党，当了总统就代表全部选民。

实际上，拜登早在接受党内提名演说（2020年8月）时便说过与推文第一句几乎一模一样的话：

While I'll be a Democratic candidate, I'll be an American president.

拜登在提名演说中承诺，要做代表全体美国人的总统，而非仅代表本党本阵营的总统（represent all of us, not just our base or our party）。这条推文也是在努力展示一种"弥合分歧，呼吁团结"的姿态，而非在自夸"我稳赢了"。

把"but I will be an American president"翻译成"我将成为美

国总统"而非"我要做全体美国人的总统",虽然赚取了流量,但却丢了陆克文所说的准确与细腻。拜登的"苦口婆心吁团结"在译文中悄然变成了"乘人之危放豪言",竟还引得国内网民群嘲,真可谓"失之毫厘,谬以千里"!

另一方面,外媒在报道中国时也屡屡迷失在翻译中。有时候,英译文貌似与中文原文对应了,但在语气语调等细微之处有意无意地走偏了。

2023年6月19日下午,国家主席习近平在北京会见美国国务卿布林肯。习近平指出,中国尊重美国的利益,不会去挑战和取代美国。同样,美国也要尊重中国,不要损害中国的正当权益。任何一方都不能按照自己的意愿塑造对方,更不能剥夺对方正当发展权利。

此次会见受到国内外广泛关注,这几句话也被外媒广泛报道转引。但是,在第三句话的翻译上,外媒与中国外交部的译法不一。

外交部译法:

Neither side should try to shape the other side by its own will, still less deprive the other side of its legitimate right to development.

《华盛顿邮报》《金融时报》等多家主流外媒这样翻译:

Neither party can shape the other according to its own wishes, let alone deprive the other of its legitimate right to development.

两种译法，两种语气，关键区别在情态动词"should"与"can"的使用。根据外交部译法，"不能……更不能……"即"不应该……更不应该……"。情态动词"should"明确体现中方的主观立场与价值判断，强调"按照自己的意愿塑造对方"与"剥夺对方正当发展权利"的非正义性，突出主观态度上的"不接受"。

外媒普遍照字面把"不能"译成"neither ... can"，与外交部译法相比，淡化了主观上的劝诫，侧重"ability"或者"possibility"，更像是在陈述一种事实：It's not possible for any side to shape the other.

情态动词关乎讲话语气，尤其是在外交语境下，情态动词的使用须仔细斟酌。比较上述两种译法可见，外交部译法在语义和语气上更忠实于原文，更能如实反映中国立场。

以上两例，一个是英翻中，一个是中翻英，都是笔者在工作实践中遇到的"在翻译中迷失"的案例。这类案例提醒国际传播工作者，要具备一定的文字敏感性与过硬的翻译功底，把文字译对译好，是传播中国、报道世界的重要前提。

有人说，翻译是遗憾的艺术。很多时候，原文的细腻微妙之处难以在译文中还原，专业译者都体会过这份遗憾。在国际传播实践中，我们一方面应认识到翻译的缺憾，但同时应时刻警惕因翻译不当造成的传播障碍甚至误解。笔者结合工作实践，浅谈实践中较易出现的三类翻译问题：隐喻的误解、夸张的误用、用典的迷失。

2.2.1 隐喻的误解

中英文有一共同点：隐喻表达无处不在。隐喻，是表达方式的创新，也是思维方式的外现。恰当的隐喻表达既凝练又形象，令人回味。中英文不约而同地把"婚姻"比作"马拉松"（Marriage is a marathon.），或许是不同文化背景的人都认识到婚姻极其考验耐性。中文俗语"贪多嚼不烂"与英文"bite off more than you can chew"好似孪生，都与嚼有关，形象生动。

中英文里有很多隐喻表达是相通相似的，这就决定了"直译"是翻译隐喻表达首先考虑的法门。比如，把"党历经革命性锻造"这一隐喻表达译成英文即可借用动词"temper"："The Party has tempered itself through revolution."。"temper"从"锻炼（金属）"之意引申开，可用于表达"以苦难磨砺人格/本领"：

> To strengthen through experience or hardship; toughen: <u>soldiers who had been tempered by combat</u>.（《美国传统词典》）

笔者在《笔尖上的文化碰撞：对外话语与翻译》一书中总结了英译隐喻表达的几种方法，但是，只总结方法还远远不够，还要在广阔的应用场景中善加运用。胸中有韬略，还要有足够的实战经验，否则无异于纸上谈兵（be an armchair expert）。实践中，英译时政话语中的隐喻表达，常常掉入三种陷阱。

直译的尴尬

由于风俗习惯、思维方式不同，中英文不乏具有各自语言特色的隐喻表达，这时候直译可能行不通，甚至闹笑话。英国《卫报》曾这样翻译"屁股坐歪了"：

> ... being <u>"crooked assed"</u>, an internet slang term for having

bias or lacking objectivity. (*The Guardian*, March 16, 2022)

"直译 + 解释"是外媒在新闻报道中翻译中国特色表达常用的处理手法。可惜,《卫报》把"屁股坐歪了(sit in the wrong spot)"理解成了"屁股变形了(crooked assed)"!

美国媒体 CNN 曾把中国时政话语中的"不怕鬼"直译成"not be afraid of ghosts",读来不知所云,令人哭笑不得。

We won't believe in heresies, be afraid of ghosts or succumb to pressure. (CNN, December 6, 2022)

"不信邪、不怕鬼"是饱含历史渊源与政治内涵的中国特色提法,译者不能简单追求字面的"忠实",要做一番寻根溯源的工作,搞清"不怕鬼"的内涵。请看党的二十大报告中的译法:

增强全党全国各族人民的志气、骨气、底气,不信邪、不怕鬼、不怕压,知难而进、迎难而上。

We must foster a firmer sense of purpose, fortitude, and self-belief in the whole Party and the Chinese people so that we cannot be swayed by fallacies, deterred by intimidation, or cowed by pressure. We must meet obstacles and difficulties head on.

胡乱直译中文隐喻表达的不止外媒。笔者曾见国内英文媒体发布的一段中英双语视频,标题如下:

中轴线·味——品一品舌尖上的非遗

A Taste of Beijing's Backbone via Time-honored Delicacies

"a taste of backbone"是多么诡异的画面啊！把"北京中轴线"翻译成"Beijing's backbone"是可以接受的，但是，当"backbone"与"taste"一词搭配起来，就显得诡异又搞笑了。译者竟丝毫未觉察译文的滑稽甚至惊悚，实在令人诧异。笔者在第一章"标题"一节中指出，起英文标题要跳出中文标题的形式羁绊，把握标题内涵才是第一位的。现把这句滑稽感十足的英文标题修改如下：

Discovering the Culinary Heritage Along Beijing's Central Axis

面对隐喻表达，译者需要从"思维方式"与"语言表达习惯"两个方面综合判断隐喻意象的取舍。比如，若是把"绿水青山就是金山银山"这句隐喻表达直译成"Green mountains are *gold mountains and silver mountains*"，效果如何？请看英国《卫报》的评价：

"In China, 'ecological civilisation' is marked by phrases with awkward English translations such as 'green mountains are gold mountains and silver mountains'." (*The Guardian*, October 16, 2021)

为何《卫报》认为把"金山银山"直译出来"awkward（别扭）"呢？因为"green *mountains* are gold *mountains* and silver *mountains*"这样的比喻方式对英文读者而言并不熟悉，且一句话重复三个"mountains"，冗余拖沓。换言之，中文的隐喻意象完全"复刻"至英文是行不通的，可以考虑在英译文中舍弃"金山银山"的意象，把"内涵（sense）"译出。比如：

我们坚持绿水青山就是金山银山的理念。(党的二十大报告)

We have acted on the idea that lucid waters and lush mountains are invaluable assets.

笔者在此特别想提醒读者，千万不要把官方文本中的译法当作"唯一标准答案"。在国际传播实践中，"绿水青山就是金山银山"这句论断应用的场景十分丰富，英文表达也要学会变通，方符合传播之道。比如，在标语或者标题中，不妨简化用词，以"Nature is our treasure""Green is gold"等替换官方译法。美国诗人罗伯特·弗洛斯特（Robert Frost）的短诗"Nothing Gold Can Stay"（1923）以"gold"喻世间的美好，感叹美好总是转瞬即逝。该诗第一句便是"Nature's first green is gold（大自然的第一抹绿珍贵无比）"。100年后的今天，人们谈论气候变化和环境保护时常常借用"green is gold"这句经典诗句，与"绿水青山就是金山银山"可谓异曲同工。

中英文里的隐喻表达，各有各的精彩。时政话语英译工作者应勤读英文，保持对英文的敏感，要看得出"a taste of backbone"的滑稽，看得出"green mountains are gold mountains and silver mountains"的别扭。同时，译者作为跨文化的"使者"，不妨透过文字外壳探视背后的文化、风俗与思维方式。试看一例：

（中国改革经过三十多年，已进入深水区，）可以说，容易的、皆大欢喜的改革已经完成了，好吃的肉都吃掉了，剩下的都是难啃的硬骨头。

译文一：It can be said that the easy part of the job has been done to the satisfaction of all. What is left are tough bones that are hard to chew.

译文二：The reforms that are easy and make everyone happy have all been completed. <u>The choice cuts have been eaten, and all that is left now is hard bone.</u>

"难啃的硬骨头"是否可以直译？"译文一"把"好吃的肉都吃掉了"省去不译，把"难啃的硬骨头"直译成"*chew tough bones*"。如何评价这一翻译思路？

译者需要回答两个问题：

1. Is it a common practice to chew bones (as a regular part of the diet) in the English-speaking world?

2. Is "chew tough bones" a common metaphor in English?

这两个问题，笔者问了 ChatGPT 与英美外籍专家，得到的答案都是"No"。"chew bones"多用在狗而非人身上，把"啃硬骨头"直译为"chew tough bones"喻"tackle a difficult or thorny problem"，并不太符合英文表达习惯。笔者更赞同译文二的处理方式，前半句"好吃的肉都吃掉了"直译处理，后半句保留"hard bone"则顺理成章，但关键是注意回避"chew"这一动词。

英译隐喻表达，不管不顾地直译是造成翻译迷失的最大原因。更滑稽的是，在英文写作中，若强行移植中文的隐喻意象，由于语言表达习惯与文化差异，很可能给英文读者一种不伦不类的感觉。

美国作家、记者何伟（Peter Hessler）曾在《纽约客》撰文，谈到中国学生在英文说理写作中爱用"但也不能因噎废食"作为过渡句（transition sentence），并且统统把这句中文隐喻表达直译出来：(But we should not) give up eating for fear of choking.

The words are a direct translation of *yinyefeishi*, a Chinese literary phrase. Over and over, I tried to explain that this sounds terrible in English. (*The New Yorker*, May 9, 2022)

在与"吃喝"毫不相干的主题英文写作中，把"因噎废食"直译出来作为起承转合的转折句，这是把中文叙事用词强行移植到英文叙事语境，好似"半路杀出个程咬金"。在英文写作中，"程咬金式过渡句"可能把读者吓一跳，滑稽感十足。比如这句：

My life is like a box of chocolates... I never know what I'm going to get, but I'm always in for a surprise... like a dead rat.

这句话把人生比作一盒巧克力，喻生活总有惊喜和期待，可最后的"like a dead rat"很是煞风景，不但滑稽搞笑，而且令人生厌。

把翻译腔代入写作，译者有时觉察不出"sounds terrible"之处，但不懂中文的英文读者读来就是另一个感觉。与其强行塞入与上下文失和的"因噎废食"，不如用地道平实的英文平稳过渡，比如：

But we should not give up on something at the slightest obstacle.

But we should not give up doing something because of the risk of failure.

面对隐喻表达，译者或者写作者免不了要在"imagery（意象）"与"tenor/sense（内涵）"之间权衡取舍，这是处理隐喻表达的"最后一公里"。走好这"最后一公里",特别考验语言敏感性和跨文化素养。

混合隐喻

英译隐喻表达,还要特别注意避免"混合隐喻(mixed metaphor)",即"把两个不太相干的隐喻意象凑在一起"。《剑桥高级学习词典》这样解释"mixed metaphor":

> when two or more metaphors are combined, <u>often producing a silly or an amusing effect</u> 《剑桥高级学习词典》

笔者举个例子,来体会一下混合隐喻的"画面失调":She's a diamond in the rough, waiting to spread her wings and soar like an eagle. 这句话先是把女孩比作"未经雕琢的宝石",随后却画风突变,以"展翅的鹰"作喻。两个隐喻意象单独使用都成立,但凑在一块有些不伦不类。

《纽约时报》等主流外媒也经常写出不太规范的混合隐喻句子,比如:

> Now, though, <u>a legal wild card has been injected</u> into his case and those of several other defendants in California and Washington State. (*The New York Times*, April 8, 2015)

"card(牌)"与"inject(注射)"是两个毫不相干的意象,二者搭配有些格格不入。《纽约时报》分管内容规范的副总编辑菲利普·科比特(Philip B. Corbett)不无讽刺地评价道:"*Block that* mixed metaphor *in the bud*！"。科比特故意写出"block in the bud"这一比较奇怪的英文搭配，意在讽刺，更自然的表达是"nip (that mixed metaphor) in the bud"。

外媒习惯直译中文隐喻表达，常常在这方面"栽跟头"。请看路透社的一段报道：

"Cathay Pacific can't just apologise every time, but should rectify heavily, establish rules and regulations, and stop the unhealthy trend from the root," it said. (Reuters, May 24, 2023)

这句话出自《人民日报》"侠客岛"针对"国泰航空歧视风波"的评论：国泰航空不能只是每次道歉，而应重拳整顿，建章立制，从根子上刹停歪风。

路透社的译文只能说"understandable（能看懂）"，并不地道，充满了译腔译调。最明显的就是"rectify heavily"这一奇怪搭配。"rectify"是及物动词，中文说"重拳"，英译时不能机械地拿副词"heavily"与"rectify"搭配。"重拳整顿"恰当的表述可以是"rectify the situation thoroughly"，或者换一种句式"make serious corrections"。

最后半句"stop the unhealthy trend from the root"是对"从根子上刹停不正之风"的简单直译，短短几个词，却包含两个意象：根子与风。

英文"unhealthy trend"与"root"凑在一块，比较奇怪，构成混合隐喻。用一句英文解释："trend" and "root" don't fit together logically.

路透社这个译例很有代表性，内藏中英文叙事方式差异。"从根子上刹停不正之风"在中文读者听来比较顺畅易懂,但若同时保留两个意象直译成英文,违和感较强。路透社这句译文虽能看懂,但从翻译的角度而言,不太合格。

英译这句隐喻表达,可以舍弃原文的部分意象,比如译为"address the problem at its root"。

再举一例。2022年7月14日,时任国务委员兼外长王毅在广西南宁接受中央媒体采访时讲了这样一句话:"中方愿本着相互尊重精神,为双边关系再把脉、再校准、再启航。"

这句话既有排比又有隐喻,且隐喻有三个:"把脉""校准""启航"。BBC、路透社等外媒把三个隐喻意象直译出来:

> The Chinese side is willing to take the pulse [on ties], recalibrate, and set sail again. (BBC, July 20, 2022)

外媒把三个隐喻意象译出,虽不影响读者理解,但"take pulse""recalibrate""set sail"三种意象有些不相干,在英文中凑在一起略显混乱,成为英文里的混合隐喻。

外交部译法舍弃隐喻意象,以三个"re-"对应中文里的三个"再",构词巧妙,在排比结构上更贴近原文,语言表达也更流畅:

> China is ready to re-examine, re-calibrate, and reinvigorate bilateral ties in the spirit of mutual respect.

然而,混合隐喻也并非一无是处。少数情况下,为了故意实现某种效果,混合隐喻也有用武之地。比如,这句"He was a lion on the battlefield, but a lamb in the bedroom."把"狮子(a lion)"与"羔羊(a lamb)"两种意象混在一起,前后形成鲜明对比。电影《社交网络》（The Social Network）里有一句巧用混合隐喻的台词：

> Sean Parker: Ah ha! You see, the shoe is on the other...
>
> Amy: Foot?
>
> Sean Parker: Table. Which has turned.

"the shoe is on the other foot"与"the table has turned"都表示"形势逆转（The situation has changed or reversed.）"，编剧把这两个短语"移花接木（The shoe is on the other table.）"，幽默感十足，令观众印象深刻。

英译隐喻表达，译者还要对中英文词语"隐喻暗示（metaphorical connotation）"的细微差异有所体会。中文里常用"狗"字骂人，因为"狗"在中文里的隐喻暗示比较负面，相比而言，英文"dog"的负面暗示就弱一些。比如，英文"underdog"可以表达"在比赛中处于劣势的一方"，并不必然带有贬义色彩，译成中文时，若把"狗"字译出，便在中译文中平添了较强的贬义色彩。把表达"监管机构"的英文单词"watchdog"译成"看门狗"，也会平添不必要的负面色彩。同样，把贬义色彩浓厚的"走狗"二字直译为"running dog"，在英文中的"杀伤力"其实已较中文少了几分。"走狗"更接近英文中的"(someone's) attack dog"，而"running dog"更容易让英文读者想到可爱的宠物狗。美国"国会山网站"（The Hill）曾这样描述前国务卿蓬佩奥与前总统特朗普的关系：

> Pompeo is Trump attack dog on China, COVID-19 (May 10, 2020)

总之，在翻译和写作实践中，处理隐喻表达"雷区密布"，隐喻意象是保留、省略抑或是转换，需要具体问题具体分析。

同时，我们还应以包容开放的眼光看待语言的发展。有些隐喻表达作为语言表达和思维方式的创新，也许一开始听起来略显奇怪，但随着时间的推移和语言的相互影响，也可能会逐渐流行开。比如，英文"shed crocodile tears"直译成"流下鳄鱼的眼泪"，早已被中文读者接受，反而没有必要处处译为"假慈悲"了。

2.2.2 夸张的误用

夸张（hyperbole）是中英文作家都爱用的修辞手法。夸张用得好，能调动读者想象力，引起共鸣，令人印象深刻。古今中外，想象力丰富的文人巨擘尤其擅长使用夸张修辞，比如：

> 白发三千丈，缘愁似个长。（李白《秋浦歌》）
> 燕山雪花大如席，片片吹落轩辕台。（李白《北风行》）
> 相顾无言，惟有泪千行。（苏轼《江城子》）

外媒写作中也十分注重"择机"使用夸张修辞。比如：

> "To me, I can understand banning TikTok at government places because those are more sensitive," she says. "But I'm not important enough as a college student <u>with eight cents to my name</u>." (BBC, March 13, 2023)

中文成语"一文不名"形容人极度穷困，英文用"with eight cents to my name（名下只有八分钱）"，异曲同工。"eight cents"是虚指，换成"three cents""five cents"效果是一样的。

> Kovac said the moment was chilling, but she calmed her nerves, took the boy by the hand and led him to the front of the classroom, where she used a phone to call 911. She then sat at Zwerner's desk holding the boy in her arms for <u>three minutes</u> until police arrived. <u>It seemed like an eternity.</u> (*The Washington Post*, August 9, 2023)

2023年初，美国一个6岁男孩开枪打伤老师，学校另一名老师艾米·科瓦克（Amy Kovac）回忆当时的场景：她来到案发现场，抱起男孩并拨打报警电话，与男孩一起等待警察到来。短短三分钟，科瓦克感觉像是漫长无尽的等待。"It seemed like an eternity."是夸张表达，表达了她内心的紧张与煎熬。

中英文很多夸张手法是相通的。宋代才子秦观把"泪"比作"春江"，既是比喻也是夸张："便作春江都是泪，流不尽，许多愁"（秦观《江城子》）。英文中也有类似表达：She cried a river of tears. 英文里把"雪花"比作"餐盘"（The snowflakes were as big as dinner plates），"诗仙"李白则更进一步，把"雪花"比作"席子"（雪花大如席）。

在中英文里觅得相通相似的夸张表达，实在是一种享受。中文成语"倾国倾城"是形容美人的夸张表达，英国汉学家邓罗（C. H. Brewitt Taylor）将其直译为"Her beauty was such as to overthrow cities and ruin states."，保留了"倾国倾城"一词的夸张力量。这样的直译在英文中是可以理解的，因为英文中有与之类似的夸张表达：the face that launched a thousand ships。希腊神话中的美女海伦，16 岁时被迫嫁给斯巴达王，成为斯巴达王后。后来特洛伊王子帕里斯到访斯巴达，把海伦拐回特洛伊。斯巴达王大怒，由此引发特洛伊战争。海伦的美使"千艘战舰齐发"，威力不比"倾国倾城"小。英国汉学家邓罗敢于直译"倾国倾城"正是因为西方文化中有与之类似的夸张表述，英文读者不会迷失在直译中。

在对外报道中使用夸张修辞，如果能贴合语境，又能融通中外语言表达习惯，自然是两全其美之道。2023 年 3 月 20 日，海关总署署长俞建华在国新办举行的发布会上表示，"海水不干，打私不断"。这句表态让笔者想到苏格兰诗人罗伯特·伯恩斯（Robert Burns）的诗：

> As fair are you, my bonnie lass,
>
> So deep in love am I,
>
> And I will love you still, my dear,
>
> Until all the seas go dry. (*A Red, Red Rose*)

英国诗人说"海水不干，爱你不止"，那么我们也完全可以把"海水不干，打私不断"直译出来：Combating smuggling will not cease as long as there is water in the sea.

但是，夸张表述要注意分寸、注意语境、注意对象，用得不好极易引起听者反感。在小说《麦田里的守望者》中，校长斯宾塞这样夸赞主人公霍尔顿的父母：They are *grand* people.

霍尔顿嘴上应和"Yes they are. They're very nice."，心里却忍不住吐槽：真讨厌"grand"这个词。这词儿太虚伪（phony）。每次听到都想吐（puke）。

用"grand"这个词形容人,这种"夸张式奉承(hyperbolic flattery)"的确有些浮夸油腻,不如简简单单的"nice"显得真诚。

在对外新闻报道中,我们尤其不能对夸张表述掉以轻心,要注意夸张的"误用"与"误读"。新闻报道以真实、客观为第一要务,而浮夸表述很可能引起霍尔顿那样的生理反应。

国内某媒体英文记者曾在报道中这样使用夸张修辞:

I left no stone unturned, but you still couldn't find any trace of violations...

BBC驻华记者史蒂芬·麦克唐纳(Stephen Mcdonell)在社交平台嘲讽: She's "left no stone unturned". Today's dose of pretty funny *propaganda*.

英文俚语"leave no stone unturned"意思是"用尽全力做某事",常用在两种语境:

"To leave no stone unturned" is an idiom that means to do everything possible to find something or to solve a problem. It is often used to praise someone's careful work or to promise a thorough search. (*The Britannica Dictionary*)

由词典释义可见,这句英文俚语常用在"夸赞他人工作做得细"或者"承诺要把工作做细"两种语境。BBC记者之所以嘲笑"leave no stone unturned"的误用,不是因为表达有语法问题,而是因为讲话者身为新闻记者,用这句夸张表达描述自身的采访调查工作,与严谨客观的新闻报道很不协调。BBC记者用充满负面色彩的"propaganda"一词讽刺,言外之意是: It's the opposite of journalism.

实践中，笔者看到很多诸如此类的误用。写作者把平日积累的"地道表达"不顾语境、不顾身份、不顾语气地移植嫁接，暗秀文采，实则贻笑大方。《纽约时报》副总编菲利普·科比特提醒记者编辑：用词克制是一种美德（Restraint is a virtue.）。请看《纽约时报》用词过分夸张的一则案例：

> That is the largest such gap, or "spread," since 1989, according to Marc Chandler, global head of currency strategy at Brown Brothers Harriman. And it has <u>unleashed a tsunami of capital flows</u> from Europe to the United States. (*The New York Times*, March 11, 2015)

科比特在《纽约时报》撰文批评自家记者滥用"tsunami"：

> Unless you're describing an actual natural disaster, metaphors like "tsunami" or "earthquake" are almost always over the top. (*The New York Times*, April 21, 2015)

科比特这篇文章的题目起得很有讽刺意味：An Unprecedented Tsunami of Hyperbole。题目中故意使用两个夸张性词语"unprecedented"与"tsunami"，旨在提醒新闻工作者要慎用夸张性表达。

《纽约时报》写作规范还特别提醒记者编辑在描述当下的事件时要慎用"historic"一词：

> Use it with caution for a current event, <u>because history's verdict is rarely predictable by journalists, and the word suggests hyperbole</u>.

纽约大学理论物理学家史蒂文·库宁（Steven E. Koonin）在《华尔街日报》发表评论文章，批评媒体、政界在气候变化议题上总是危言耸听，"climate hell""last, best chance to save the planet""hellish future"等夸张表述不绝于耳。库宁认为，形势远远没有这些夸张词描述得那么严峻。文章标题故意用词夸张（a flood of），很有讽刺意味：Climate Change Brings a Flood of Hyperbole（*The Wall Street Journal*, August 10, 2021）。库宁曾在奥巴马政府担任能源部副部长，其"全球变暖尚无定论"的观点也不乏批评者。

在国际传播实践中，我们要对中文里的夸张表达保持警惕，尤其要意识到：把中式夸张表达贸然直译成英文，很可能引起不适，甚至误读。一位英国改稿专家读到美国《外交》杂志发布的一段英译文，对最后一句表示费解：

Our army is famous for being good at fighting and having a strong fighting spirit. With millet and rifles, it defeated the Kuomintang army equipped with American equipment. It defeated the world's number one enemy armed to the teeth on the Korean battlefield, and performed might and majestic battle dramas that shocked the world and caused ghosts and gods to weep. (*Foreign Affairs*, March 29, 2023)

我军素以能征善战、有强大战斗精神闻名于世，以小米加步枪打败了美式装备的国民党军队，在朝鲜战场打败了武装到牙齿的世界头号强敌，演出了一幕幕威武雄壮的战争活剧，创造了一个个惊天地、泣鬼神的英雄壮举。

"惊天地、泣鬼神"既是夸张也是用典，语出杜甫《寄李太白二十韵》："笔落惊风雨，诗成泣鬼神。"这句夸张表达为国人熟知，表达"可歌可泣""震撼人心"之意，但是直译成"caused ghosts and gods to weep"一定会令广大英文读者茫然不解甚至胡思乱想。英国外专问笔者：这句话想表达什么意思？有何深意吗？为何中文要这样表达？

笔者告诉外专，"泣鬼神"源自唐诗，常与"惊天地"一起搭配，增强表达效果，并无特殊深意。用在时政话语中，"泣鬼神"是一种夸张表达，意思是"to achieve a *stunning* victory / perform an *amazing* feat"。

外专继续问：那为何不用简单直白的语言表达呢？如果英文读者读不懂文字的内涵，又如何读懂中国呢？

英国外专的疑问很有代表性，又回到了哈佛大学教授、中国问题专家安东尼·赛奇对中英文叙事方式差异的提醒："中文的叙事方式在中国很受欢迎，但在说英语的地方就不那么受欢迎了。"

有些措辞与形式，在中文里是文采斐然，强行移植到英文可能就显得累赘冗余，甚至格格不入。格格不入的，常常并非"内容"本身，而是"表达形式"，也许就是贸然出现了"ghosts and gods weep"这样的直译，或者多用了几个像"grand"这般浮夸的修饰词，便足以拒人于千里之外。

国际传播工作者应时刻谨记中英叙事方式的巨大差异，勤阅读、广涉猎，保持语言敏感。既然我们有志于打造融通中外的新概念、新范畴、新表述，就不能不重视语言的细节。本该是对外表达的内容，但语言、形式和逻辑却还是"对内"的，结果引起目标受众反感。如果我们的对外表述总是给英文读者"sounds like propaganda"之感，那么，融通中外不就成为一句空话了吗？

2.2.3 用典的问题

中英文都不乏用典修辞（allusion）。典故用得好，自然浑成，省却千言万语。用典之妙，恰如欧阳修所言：状难写之景如在目前，含不尽之意见于言外。

英国《卫报》在报道中澳关系时，悄无声息地引用莎士比亚名句：

Yet this rhetorical sound and fury signifies little for Australia-China ties. Although Beijing will continue to oppose Aukus, China is unlikely to reverse the bilateral relationship repair of recent months. (*The Guardian*, May 15, 2023)

"sound and fury signifies little"化用了莎士比亚悲剧《麦克白》中的名句。

Life's but a walking shadow, a poor player

That struts and frets his hour upon the stage,

And then is heard no more. It is a tale

Told by an idiot, full of sound and fury,

Signifying nothing.

人生不过是一个行走的影子，

一个在舞台上指手划脚的拙劣的伶人，

登场片刻，就在无声无臭中悄然退下；

它是一个愚人所讲的故事，

充满着喧哗和骚动，

却找不到一点意义。

（朱生豪 译）

在不制造阅读障碍的前提下，善于用典，给文字增加一点文采，何乐而不为？

2022年9月9日，英国查尔斯国王发表首次电视讲话，悼念母亲伊丽莎白二世。演讲结尾，查尔斯引用莎翁名句抚慰逝者安息：

Thank you for your love and devotion to our family and to the family of nations you have served so diligently all these years. May flights of angels sing thee to thy rest.

最后一句出自莎士比亚悲剧《哈姆雷特》，"thee"是古英语"you"，"thy"是古英语"your"。在悲剧最后一幕，哈姆雷特（Hamlet）中毒身亡，在好友霍拉旭（Horatio）的怀中逝去。霍拉旭悲痛地说：

Now cracks a noble heart. Good night, sweet prince. And flights of angels sing thee to thy rest.

一颗高贵的心现在碎裂了！晚安，亲爱的王子，愿成群的天使们用歌唱抚慰你安息。（朱生豪 译）

在现代英语中，"May flights of angels sing thee to thy rest"这句古语依然广泛使用，相比"Rest in peace（RIP）"感情更浓烈。

无论是外媒编辑部，还是英美政府高层写作班子，都不约而同地引用莎翁名句，可见莎士比亚在英文世界的影响力。正如中国人表达思乡，几乎都会吟诵李白的诗句——"举头望明月，低头思故乡"。

用典虽妙，但也有潜在风险。英国前首相鲍里斯·约翰逊在离任演说中自比古罗马政客辛辛那提（Cincinnatus）：

Like Cincinnatus, I am returning to my plough.

"plough"就是耕地用的犁，"return to my plough"便是"解甲归田"之意。

辛辛那提何许人也？公元前5世纪，罗马军队遭意大利埃奎人包围，危难之际，罗马高层请求正在务农的辛辛那提出山力挽狂澜。辛辛那提不辱使命，且退敌不久便主动解甲归田。

可是，历史并非这般简单，历史人物也绝非几笔粗线条可以勾勒。辛辛那提后来再次掌权，成为漠视民众权利的独裁者。因此，英国《卫报》不无讽刺地写道：

Boris Johnson likens himself to Roman <u>who returned as dictator</u>. (*The Guardian*, September 6, 2022)

退下去的约翰逊自比辛辛那提，而美国佛罗里达州州长德桑蒂斯（Ron DeSantis）在接受福克斯新闻网专访时把美国总统拜登比作古罗马暴君尼禄：Biden is the American Nero.

同样，对尼禄的评价，史家也有争议。美国媒体《纽约客》曾撰文为尼禄打抱不平，标题是"How nasty was Nero, really?"。文章认为，尼禄的恶名乃是对后世君主的污蔑。

Not for the last time, the celebration of a new emperor entailed the disfiguring of Nero. (*The New Yorker*, June 7, 2021)

中外历史上，每逢王朝更替，新王朝史官修史，免不了要对前朝的人和事扭曲贬低。《纽约时报》有一篇评论文章曾这样论历史学家的责任，笔者以为说得好极了。请看：

The proper role of the historian is to complexify, not simplify; to show us historical figures in the context of their time, not reduce them to figurines that can be weaponized in our contemporary debates. (*The New York Times*, August 30, 2022)

历史学家应发挥这样的角色：呈现历史的复杂，而非简化历史。把历史人物置于时代背景中去展示，而非把历史人物脸谱化，沦为当下辩论的武器。

把历史人物脸谱化，虽然方便叙事，但不利于看清历史真面目。严肃的史家常常用警惕的目光审视粗线条的历史叙事。约翰逊自比辛辛那提，反遭英媒群嘲，看来英文用典也须格外谨慎。

观欧美政客与外媒用典，对我们在国际传播工作中做好中文典故英译具有重要的启示意义。用典之妙得以彰显，须以写作者/讲话者与受众之间拥有共同的语言和文化背景为基础。

无论中文还是英文，用典应兼顾"2R"原则：对目标受众而言，用典要清晰易懂（Readable）；对文本语境而言，用典要有的放矢（Relevant），恰到好处。

如果用典隐晦难懂，好似迷雾烟瘴，抑或是为了"掉书袋"而用典，便失去了用典的意义，也不利于传播。举一个比较"极端"的反面案例：2021年11月2日，马斯克（Elon Musk）在自己的推特（今名"X"）账号发布一条推文，其"无厘头"般用典，令全球网民大感费解。请看：

Humankind

煮豆燃豆萁

豆在釜中泣

本是同根生

相煎何太急

马斯克引用曹植的《七步诗》，并以"Humankind（人类）"一词为标题，究竟想表达什么？有人猜马斯克是在说全球粮食问题，有人猜是与比特币有关，还有人猜是在向中国示好。五花八门的猜测，引得《华盛顿邮报》、路透社、CNN等各路媒体报道，但最终也无定论。

在英文中引用中文典故有诸多陷阱。由于中西方思维方式与文化背景不同，中文典故背后的精神内涵很容易在英文中迷失。主要体现在两个方面：

（1）在直译中迷失（Nuances are easily lost.）。约翰逊和德桑蒂斯在同一文化语境下用典尚且存在误读的风险，在跨文化语境下，把一种文化里的元素符号直译到另一种文化里，元素符号承载的象征意义以及细腻幽深之处很可能无法顺利传递。"惊天地、泣鬼神"既是夸张也是用典，直译后令一般英文读者大惑不解。中国人习惯以雪中梅花（plum blossom in the snow）喻不屈不挠、坚韧不拔的品质。王安石有诗云：墙角数枝梅，凌寒独自开。但英文读者未必熟悉这样的象征。2022年1月4日，习近平总书记在北京考察冬奥会、冬残奥会筹办工作时，用"不经一番寒彻骨，怎得梅花扑鼻香"勉励备战冬奥的运动员们。

"Only those who withstand the freezing cold could enjoy the fragrance of plum blossom," Xi quoted a poem to encourage the athletes to cherish the precious opportunity after years of preparations for sporting excellence. (Xinhua, January 5, 2022)

为什么引用"梅花"诗句？梅花在中国文化中有何象征意义？如果不把这些交代一下，一般英文读者恐怕难以细察用典的深意。在对外报道中，不妨补充交代一句"梅花"的象征意义：In Chinese culture, the plum blossom is a symbol of courage, perseverance, and triumph over adversity, as it blooms in the harsh winter.

当我们把"天人合一"引入当代政治话语，阐释人与自然和谐共生的内在规律和本质要求，把"天"字直译成"heaven"不如译成"nature"更贴切，更有现实意义。

"天人合一"思想

harmony between humanity and nature（《习近平谈治国理政》第四卷英文版）

（2）在过度意译中"误入歧途"（Cultural sensitivity matters.）。英译中文典故，要警惕意译过了头而掉入译入语文化陷阱。比如，把"愚公移山"精神译成"Faith can move mountains."，貌似简洁地道，实则已入歧途。这句"Faith can move mountains."有比较明显的基督教色彩（biblical connotation），源自《圣经》里的一段话：

> Truly I tell you, if you have <u>faith</u> as small as a mustard seed, you can say to this <u>mountain, "Move from here to there," and it will move.</u> (Matthew 17:20)

此处的"faith"并非世俗意义上的"confidence in ourselves"，而是指"faith in God"。《圣经》里说：哪怕对神的信仰仅有芥菜籽那么大点儿，也可有移山之力。《圣经》中的另一句可作为"Faith can move mountains."的注解：

> <u>For with God</u> nothing shall be impossible. (Luke 1:37)

"愚公移山"精神指的是苦干实干精神，表达了"精神一到，何事不成"的决心与信心，与基督教里"信神则无事不成"完全是两码事。英译中文典故，切不可"捡了芝麻丢了西瓜"，为了文字地道而损伤甚至改变精神内涵。可以把"faith"改为"perseverance"：Perseverance can move mountains.

中国历史文化悠久，因此典故极其丰富。然而，并非所有的典故都适合对外传播，要善于在经典中发现中外文化的共通之处，以及典故中蕴含的当下现实意义。这既需要敏锐的跨文化意识，也需要一点奇思妙想。

《经济学人》报道中美经贸关系，曾在标题中化用中文成语"卧虎藏龙（crouching tiger, hidden dragon）"，既切题又简单易懂，值得学习。请看：

> *Rising tigers, hidden dragon*
> How America is failing to break up with China (*The*

Economist, August 8, 2023）

"rising tigers"指的是美国搞"友岸外包（friendshoring）"的对象国，比如印度、墨西哥、越南等；"hidden dragon"自然指的是中国。标题里的"failing to break up with China"又是浪漫的隐喻：中美关系史好似曲折复杂的爱恨情仇史，想说分手不容易。标题兼具用典和隐喻，足见编辑用心。

英国作家祁立天（Tim Clissold）从《卖炭翁》等现实主义古诗词中读出了当下意义，因为很多经典内容虽然历经千年，依然是当下的英文读者可以理解乃至共情的。祁立天在接受央视国际频道（CGTN）连线采访时说，在西方社会，有（对华）鹰派也有鸽派。但鹰鸽两派有一个共识：都需要更好地了解和认识中国。在他看来，中国古诗中蕴含的现实启示以及折射的思想光辉，如友情、人与自然的关系等，依然是21世纪的英文读者可以感同身受的。[1]

2021年，英国作家、汉学家蓝诗玲"改写+翻译"了《西游记》。在英译本的"翻译絮语"一节中，蓝诗玲坦言，为了叙事方便和节奏流畅，不得不舍弃原文中大量的诗词、双关语、顺口溜等。如果纯粹去"翻译"《西游记》，那就不得不做大量的注释和阐释工作，而以"改写+翻译"的方式更方便现代英文读者感受原著的"活力（dynamism）""想象力（imagination）""哲思（philosophy）"与"趣味（comedy）"。蓝诗玲这样概括她的"翻译观"：

---

[1] https://news.cgtn.com/news/2022-04-12/What-can-ancient-Chinese-poems-tell-us-about-the-problems-of-today--19aIyIgGD2U/index.html

Sometimes, a translator has to sacrifice technical, linguistic fidelity to be true to the overall tone of a text.

祁立天对中国古诗的解读让我们看到，中国文化里从来不缺具有"当下意义"且容易被英文读者理解的元素，关键是要善于挖掘。蓝诗玲用英文讲《西游记》的思路和技巧给我们很多启示：对于中国文化中难讲难懂的元素，要有"舍"与"得"的意识，有时需要"舍"弃文字层面的忠实，求"得"整体风格的再现。这样或许可以让中国文化对外传播取得更好的效果。

第三章 国际传播：困境与突破

3.1 文化差异

"中国最后一位儒家"梁漱溟先生比较中西文化差异，认为中国社会结构是"伦理本位"，以欧美为代表的西方则是"个人本位"。"伦理本位之重点，乃在相关系之两方中之对方。……伦理关系，亦即是相互间之义务关系。……每个中国人必须各自认识其义务而履行之，却从来不许谈权利。……凡讲权者皆以自我为中心。而伦理则看重对方也。"（《中国文化的命运》）

"修昔底德陷阱"提出者、哈佛大学教授格雷厄姆·艾利森（Graham Allison）在其专著《注定一战：中美能避免修昔底德陷阱吗？》一书中从"自我定位""核心价值""政府观"等多个维度对比了中美之间的文化碰撞。在艾利森看来，美国的核心价值是自由（freedom），中国的核心价值是秩序（order）。新加坡学者马凯硕在《中国的选择》一书中也曾给出类似的结论：中国文化注重社会和谐（social harmony）。美国文化恰恰相反，更重视个体赋权（individual empowerment）。

马凯硕进一步提醒读者，混乱无序（chaos）本应是国家软弱（weakness）的体现，但在美国反而是强大（strength）的体现。

中国文化历来讲和谐，不喜乱哄哄；西方恰恰相反，公民的不服从与社会的喧闹反而司空见惯。鲜有机会接触西方文化的一些网民，每每见到西方社会的争吵与喧闹，常常不解、不屑甚至嘲讽。

国际传播工作者面临中西两个世界，两种舆论场，对核心价值观冲突感受最直接，因为价值冲突绝不是一句空谈，而会反映在一个又一个具体的新闻事件中。

2021年8月，国家新闻出版署印发《关于进一步严格管理 切实防止未成年人沉迷网络游戏的通知》。根据通知要求，所有网络游戏企业仅可在周五、周六、周日和法定节假日每日的20时至21时向未成年人提供1小时服务，其他时间一律不得向未成年人提供网络游戏服务。

"限游令"在国内舆论场受到广泛好评，同时也受到主流外媒关注，引起国外网民热议。笔者从外媒文章以及海外社交媒体X（原名"推特"）、TikTok留言区的讨论中观察到，欧美网民对"限游令"的负面评价要远远多于正面评价。很多外国网民认为"政府管得太宽了"，有的甚至惊呼"That's frightening."。同一件事，国内外舆论可谓"冰火两重天"。此类新闻不断提醒国际传播工作者，在对外报道中，要善于从文化差异的视角对选题进行预判，我们拿到国际舆论场上的、引以为豪的素材是否有说服力，是否能实现预期的效果，不能想当然。西方民众以西方视角看中国常常看不懂，我们如果习惯以自己的想象或者思维惯性去评判一个文化迥异的彼岸，也容易看不清。只有从文化内核入手，明晰彼此差异，进而发出的声音才可能有回响。

对欧美"个人主义"核心价值观，我们要辩证地看。美国最高法院前大法官约翰·马歇尔·哈伦（John Marshall Harlan）在一个经典司法判例中写道："美国政治体系的基石是个体的尊严与选择自由。"这一基石对西方经济社会的繁荣发展功不可没，但弊端缺陷也十分明显。新冠疫情早期，我们看到，无论是政府强推戴口罩还是鼓励打疫苗，都遭到不少西方民众近乎顽固的抵抗。我们看到，时任纽约州州长安德鲁·科莫（Andrew Cuomo）与时任美国总统特朗普隔空互怼，这与强调"全国一盘棋"，强调"团结一心""稳定有序"的政治文化形成鲜明对比。

2021年11月，美国前劳工部长、加州大学伯克利分校公共政策教授罗伯特·赖希（Robert Reich）在英国《卫报》撰文，分析美国疫苗接种率较低的原因。赖希从美国民众对"大药企""大政府"的不信任等表层原因直指最深层的文化原因，即，国民"性格特征（character trait）"。

> In fact, I think this trait has been near the core of the American personality since before the founding of the nation – a stubborn, selfish, me-first individualism. (*The Guardian*, November 28, 2021)
>
> 从美国建国以前直至今天，这一特征一直是美国人性格特征的内核：顽固、自私、自我至上的个人主义。

赖希的概括可谓"稳、准、狠"，自我鞭挞，入木三分。

"伦理本位"文化熏陶下的国民性格必然与"个人本位"文化熏陶下的国民性格大不相同。中美防疫政策与效果的差异，可追根溯源至中美文化与人民性格的差异。潘岳先生在《中西文明根性比较》一书中说得透彻：两种文明根性塑造了两种不同的道路。西方不断走向分，最终归结到了个人主义和自由主义。中国则不断走向合，造就了中华文明的集体主义根性。当今时代，最大的矛盾是"自由优先"还是"秩序优先"。

在这个多元与矛盾并存的世界，与其陷入无尽的争吵与对立，不如以"中庸"视角看待价值位阶排序。正如潘岳在书中结尾所呼吁的：对于自由来说，要探讨如何加强秩序，以防止瓦解；对于秩序来说，要探讨如何加强自由，以激发创新。问题不是如何在自由与秩序中二选一，而是在哪个环节加强自由，在哪个环节加强秩序。

3.2 身份困境

"限游令"在中外舆论场获得截然相反的反应，让我们不得不正视国际传播工作中最棘手的价值观差异："政府观"差异。

美国开国元勋托马斯·潘恩有句名言：政府，即便是最佳状态，也只是必要之恶（a necessary evil）。美国前总统里根在1981年的就职演说中有这样一句话：

> Government is not the solution to our problem; government is the problem.

> 政府不是解决问题的方法，政府本身就是问题。

在笔者看来，里根这句话或许是受到美国作家、哲学家亨利·梭罗的启发。梭罗在《论公民的不服从》（On the Duty of Civil Disobedience）一书中写道：

> Government is at best but an expedient; but most governments are usually, and all governments are sometimes, inexpedient.

> 政府充其量也只是（解决问题的）权宜之计罢了。大多数政府在多数时候，所有政府在有些时候，恰恰是不合理的。

实际上，梭罗在书中开篇第一句话就亮明了观点：我打心底里认同这句格言——管得最少的政府就是最好的政府。从潘恩到梭罗，再到里根，我们能清晰地看到一脉相承的"政府观"。

与之相反，正如哈佛大学教授艾利森所指出的，中国民众视政府为"必要之善（a necessary good）"。新加坡南洋理工大学经济学教授陈光炎（Tan Kong Yam）从经济学视角对中西"政府观"差异有深刻的观察：

> Unlike the Euro-American model that traces its origin to the tradition of Adam Smith, which treats government as <u>a necessary evil</u> that should be confined to only law and order, Confucian values and tradition lead to a model of <u>maximal government</u>, with myriad responsibilities, duties, and obligations. The state is not just supervisory and regulatory in function, <u>but plays a leadership role</u> in development, education, and mobilization behind specific priorities.
>
> 欧美模式可追溯至亚当·斯密古典传统：视政府为必要之恶，政府须受法律与秩序约束。与欧美模式不同，儒家观念与传统塑造了"大政府"模式：政府肩负无数责任、义务与职责。政府不仅仅行使监督和监管职能，还在发展、教育以及动员力量推动特定事业发展等方面发挥领导角色。

中国的历史和文化决定了人们历来对政府寄予厚望，希望政府有力、有为、有效。在欧美的"政府观"影响下，西方社会对"政府权力扩张的警惕"要甚于"对政府效率的追求"。

2022年9月6日，中央全面深化改革委员会第二十七次会议指出，健全关键核心技术攻关新型举国体制，要把政府、市场、社会有机结合起来，科学统筹、集中力量、优化机制、协同攻关。

2022年9月14日，英国国际战略研究所（IISS）特别顾问奈杰尔·因克斯特（Nigel Inkster）在《纽约时报》撰文指出：

<u>Mobilizing government, society and economic and academic systems</u> around competition with foreign foes the way China does would <u>betray Western values</u>. (*The New York Times*, September 14, 2022)

像中国那样把政府、社会以及经济和学术系统等方面动员起来与外敌竞争，（这种做法）是背离西方价值观的。

对照着看，不难发现中西方在政府角色、"政府观"等方面的差异不啻天壤。反映到对外讲好中国故事的具体实践中，中西"政府观"差异的影响也是实实在在的。

在海外社交平台，具有政府背景的中外媒体曾一度被特别标注身份属性。英国广播公司（BBC）、美国全国公共广播电台（NPR）等受西方政府资助的媒体，都曾被打上"国家附属媒体""政府资助"等标签。NPR 对"打标签"行为表示抗议，称资金来源只有 1% 来自美国联邦政府，"打标签"有损其客观独立之形象。NPR 于 2023 年 4 月 12 日愤然退出推特平台。BBC 也对"打标签"一事提出抗议。推特老板马斯克（Elon Musk）在回应 BBC 的抗议时说："在我看来，BBC 其实并不像其他一些政府资助的媒体那样充满偏见，但是，BBC 宣称'零政府影响'是愚蠢的。说 BBC 受到'些许政府影响（minor government influence）'是准确的。"

给媒体"打标签"，其实反映了西方社会对政府之声的高度警惕。BBC、NPR 在欧美国家都难逃警惕的眼神，可想而知，中国官方媒体和官媒记者的声音很容易被视为"别有目的的宣传（propaganda）"，哪怕讲的内容只是熊猫与长城。

2021 年，阿里巴巴集团高管蔡崇信接受美国财经媒体 CNBC 专访，被记者问及中国香港、人权等尖锐问题。蔡崇信从鸦片战争、生存权、发展权等角度用英文回答，很多海外网民给他的回答点赞。不少国内网民看了访谈片段，也纷纷点赞。有的网民甚至留言疾呼：国际传播就该这么讲话才对嘛！但是，在许多国际传播一线工作者看来，蔡崇信的回答在内容上并无多少创新之处，同样的话，同样的逻辑，国家英文媒体以文字或视频的形式对外讲了何止百次千次。不同之处是，蔡崇信是非官方的企业家。

目前，中国的国际传播主力依然是官方，由中西"政府观"差异所造成的身份困境是无论如何也绕不开的"拦路虎"。很多时候"讲故事的人（storyteller）"比"故事（story）"本身更受关注，对此我们要有深刻的理解。

3.3 突破之道

首先回答一个问题：中国的国际传播面临怎样的外部舆论环境？

英国剑桥大学 2022 年发布的一项调查报告显示：在采用西方政治制度模式的国家中（人口大约 12 亿），75% 的人对中国持负面看法；但是，在全球 136 个非西方式民主国家的约 63 亿人口中，70% 的人对中国持正面看法。[1]

这是一个喜忧参半的结论。喜的是，从全球范围来看，中国越来越赢得发展中国家民众的好感。忧的是，西方舆论对中国的好感度在下降。有人说，不能把西方舆论等同于国际舆论。这话有道理，但同时我们也应该清醒地认识到，西方国家仍然掌握着国际舆论的主导权，握着最大的"麦克风"。换言之，（对华好感的）人口优势还不能转化成话语优势。

英国汉学家克里·布朗认为，中国故事的外部受众有两个特点：（1）对中国的国情、历史和文化知之甚少；（2）对中国的政治制度抱有强烈的敌意。基于这两个特点，中国叙事面临三种反应：（1）全盘接受（utter acceptance），如巴基斯坦；（2）深深的怀疑（deep skepticism），如欧洲；（3）满满的敌意（outright hostility），如美国和印度。（《海牙外交学研究》）

思考国际传播的突破之道，不能无视这一现实话语格局，否则容易陷入盲目自大而不自知。

---

[1] https://www.cam.ac.uk/stories/worlddivided

3.3.1 谁来讲

笔者认为，我们寻求突破之道，首先要树立一个意识：Storytellers matter（谁来讲很重要）。在对外传播实践中，我们常常只关注"讲什么"的问题，而轻视"谁来讲"的问题。这种认知惰性背后也许存在一种错误的惯性思维：国际传播只是官方媒体等官方机构的事。

诚然，目前国际传播的主力依然是官方，但对外讲好中国故事不仅是官方的事情，也是每个中国人的事情。中国故事要在流量和公信力上取得进一步突破，应鼓励更多的非官方个体参与中国叙事。

英国汉学家克里·布朗认为：

> On the question of who tells the story beside the Chinese state, there can be some flexibility. Chinese students, tourists, businesspeople, artistic figures and the public can all take part in this grand act of storytelling and contribute their own specific narratives. In some ways, the more this happens, the more the story becomes human, and the more palatable it is likely to be outside of China's borders. (《海牙外交学研究》)

在官方之外谁来讲这个问题上，可以存在一定的灵活变通。学生、游客、商人、艺术界人士、公众都可以参与到讲好中国故事这一宏大实践，贡献他们的叙事。在某种程度上，他们参与得越多，中国故事越有人情味，也越容易被海外受众喜欢。

注意"human（富有人情味的）"这个形容词。关心国际传播工作的中外人士都在不断提醒，要把故事讲得有人情味、有感染力，因为宏大严肃的叙事、粗线条的描摹太朦胧太生硬，不是讲故事之道。但我们别忘了把目光"前移"，在关注"故事"本身的同时，多看看"讲故事的人"。非官方身份的讲述者更容易突破价值观隔阂与广大受众共情，讲故事的主体越多元，中国故事越有人情味，也越容易被海外受众喜欢。

中国外文局原副局长兼总编辑黄友义先生在《从"翻译世界"到"翻译中国"：对外传播与翻译实践文集》一书中多次强调"公共外交/全民外交"的概念，提出每一个有机会接触到外国人的中国人都要担负起传播中国的责任。传播与文化交流无时不在发生，走出国门的中国人已经在透过自身的言行举止"翻译"中国。

欧美私有化媒体都特别注重在故事中体现"人情味"，不只做硬新闻，更擅长讲"暖故事"。《今日美国》电视频道官方简介中有一个关键词："heartwarming human moments"。

> From the nation's news to heartwarming human moments, sports, and pop culture, stay connected to the world around you with USA Today.

美国广播公司（ABC）旗下有一个全国性电视频道，名叫Localish。据官网介绍，Localish致力于讲好美国民间"正能量故事（positive stories）"。具体而言，着力讲好"三好"故事："Good food, Good people, Good living"。

把"美食"放在第一位，真应了中国那句古话——"民以食为天"。在Localish频道，观众能看到形形色色有趣的人，比如蛋糕店主、老爷车收藏爱好者、用咖啡创作的艺术家，还能一窥各式各样有趣的生活方式，感受人生的多元与精彩。

韩国电视剧《请回答1988》用一个又一个的"暖心瞬间"讲友情、亲情、爱情，不但在韩国创下了收视纪录，也征服了全球万千观众。美国媒体《纽约客》用三个词总结该剧成功的密码：搞怪的幽默、怀旧的基调、超越国界的视角。

对外讲好中国的"三好"故事，也必须找到"超越国界的视角"。人类虽有文化差异与政治分歧，但人性毕竟是相通的，所谓"人同此心，心同此理"。中国从来不缺"三好"故事素材，缺的是讲好"三好"故事的意识与技巧，以及突破国家传播、政府传播主体范畴的勇气。讲故事的主体越多元，故事越有人情味，也越容易打动世界。

3.3.2 "话语权"再思考

党的二十大报告提出：加强国际传播能力建设，全面提升国际传播效能，形成同我国综合国力和国际地位相匹配的国际话语权。

什么是"话语权（discourse power）"？从中外对这一概念不同的译法上，我们似乎能窥探到围绕这一概念的认知差异。国内习惯把"增强国际话语权"翻译为：

> make China's voice better heard
>
> amplify China's voice on the international stage

美国《外交官》杂志（The Diplomat）对"话语权"有不同的定义：

China's discourse power – the ability to set and shape global narratives – is quietly on the rise. (November 24, 2021)

中国的话语权，即，设定和左右全球叙事的能力，在悄然提升。

外媒显然认为，中国所谓的"增强国际话语权"，就是要增强"设定和左右全球叙事"的能力，而非仅仅"在国际舞台放大中国音量"。

话语权是国家软实力的体现，软实力又是综合国力的一部分。中国作为全球第二大经济体，综合国力和国际地位不可谓不显著，外界关注中国、聆听中国的欲望不可谓不强烈。截至2023年7月，美国智库战略与国际研究中心（CSIS）"解读：中国"翻译项目以及美国非营利研究机构"战略翻译中心"已全文翻译中国领导人讲话、重磅文章400余篇。与此同时，主流外媒对中国的报道愈发深入细致，国情、社情、民情均进入其报道视野。

在这样的时代背景下，解决中国声音在国际舞台"音量大不大""听不听得到"的问题其实相对容易些，难点在于中国声音在国际舞台"有没有说服力""听不听得进"，否则增强话语权便无从谈起。提升国际传播"效能"也应该朝着这个方向努力。

牛津大学中国研究中心主任、中国政治与历史学教授拉纳·米特（Rana Mitter）曾在《卫报》撰文（2022–7–17），对比中美软实力差异。米特认为，中国走中国特色社会主义道路，"特色"就意味着唯一适用性（suit no other state），但中国同时主张为世界贡献中国智慧。美国的软实力源自这样一种理念，即，理论上，任何人只要接受美国文化与价值观，均可成为美国人。

米特的评论给国际传播工作者提出一个课题：如何处理"中国特色"与"融通中外"这对关系。

曾有读者在笔者的微信公众号"外宣微记"留言：既然中西方政治文化有那么大差异乃至对立，国际传播还讲什么内外有别！

此类声音在国内不乏拥趸，但笔者并不认同，因为其逻辑本质是"Might is right（强权即公理）"。所谓"内外有别"，并非指国内报一套，国外报一套，也并非要拿一套话语去迎合或者压服另一套话语，在如今的网络时代，也不可能做到这一点。内外有别，更多的是一种"融通"意识，是在深刻认识价值观差异、话语与叙事差异的基础上，有技巧有策略地开展对外传播。相反，枉顾内外有别，不顾"特色"能否"融通"，强推硬灌，结果只能适得其反。

毛泽东同志这样谈说服的艺术："要人家服，只能说服，不能压服。压服的结果总是压而不服。以力服人是不行的。对付敌人可以这样，对付同志，对付朋友，绝不能用这个方法。"（在中国共产党全国宣传工作会议上的讲话，1957-3-12）国际传播工作是长线工作，不管国际局势如何风云变幻，国际传播的受众主体始终在民间。要实现"广交朋友、团结和争取大多数，不断扩大知华友华的国际舆论朋友圈"这一既定目标，就不能不讲究说服的艺术。

2022年，抖音海外版TikTok在英国因"文化冲突"导致员工密集离职，TikTok伦敦电商业务负责人甚至发表"公司不应提供产假"的言论，进一步激怒了本土员工。《金融时报》等英国媒体以"toxic（有毒）"一词描述这样的企业文化。这是企业枉顾文化差异的负面案例。企业要走出去、走得远，不能不考虑文化差异，中国故事讲出去若不考虑文化差异，也可能惹人厌。

在话语和叙事层面，枉顾内外有别造成的负面影响更深远。笔者在工作实践中常常遇到的一个比较"愁人"的现象：把逐句翻译当成"讲好中国故事"的方法，只粗浅地掌握"信达雅"三字诀，不懂中英文叙事差异，不懂讲故事之道，译出来的文字生硬笨拙，令人反感。

早在1967年，新西兰共产党总书记威尔科克斯（Vic Wilcox）给中国的外宣工作提出如下意见："内容很好，但所采用的语言和形式，与英语国家的群众格格不入，易引起反感。"毛泽东同志针对威尔科克斯的意见写了一句批语：一般地说，一切外国党（马列主义）的内政，我们不应干涉。他们怎样宣传，是他们的事。我们应注意自己的宣传，不应吹得太多，不应说得不适当，使人看起来好像有强加于人的印象。（《毛泽东文集》第八卷）

真正树立内外有别的意识，才能在"内容、语言和形式"这一对外表达的实践层面避免蛮干硬干。这其实也是增强国际话语权的题中之意。正如《外交官》杂志所言：在实践层面，话语权必然要求在国际舞台构建可以提升中国形象的共同语汇。

In practice, discourse power entails creating shared vocabularies in the international realm that elevate China to a more favorable position. (*The Diplomat,* November 24, 2021)

"构建共同语汇（create shared vocabularies）"不就是我们说的"打造融通中外的新概念、新范畴、新表述"吗？

今天的国际传播工作者或许应该向晚清中美文化交流的先行

者戈鲲化学习。1879 年，戈鲲化被哈佛大学聘为中文教师，成为中国赴美教学第一人。当年的哈佛大学神学院院长埃弗里特（C. C. Everett）这样称赞戈鲲化：

> He studied our Christian scriptures earnestly and reverently; but what he found in them to accept he knew how to translate into the language of his own philosophy and religion. It was such traits as these that in part won for him so many hearts. (Xu Guoqi, *Chinese and Americans: A Shared History*)
>
> 戈鲲化认真虔诚地研习基督教经典，对于经典中他所认同的内容，他懂得如何将其转化成自己的哲学和宗教语言。正是诸如这样的品质，让他广受欢迎。

戈鲲化研读西方文化经典，从中发现中西文化共通之处，并能将西方理念转化成中国化表达。今天的国际传播工作者也应勤习中西经典，磨炼把中国特色概念转化成全球化表达的本领。须知，推进中国故事的全球化表达，这话说来轻巧，但做起来一点也不容易。

第四章
ChatGPT：机遇与挑战

4.1 ChatGPT 与时政话语英译

ChatGPT，全称"Chat Generative Pre-trained Transformer（聊天生成式预训练转换模型）"，自 2022 年 11 月问世以来，已经给诸多行业带来了实实在在的变革。翻译工作者，尤其是中国时政话语英译工作者，可谓忧喜参半。忧的是，越来越多的人开始轻言"机器取代人工译者"，让翻译这一古老又迷人的行业进一步受到轻视。喜的是，以 ChatGPT 为代表的生成式人工智能在某种程度上颠覆了语言学习传统模式，其"囊括四海"的知识储备大大提高了译者解决语言难题的效率。同时，ChatGPT 可根据使用者的提问（text prompt）互动对话，按指令调整、润色译文，展现出非凡的"译后编辑（post editing）"能力。

知名网络调研公司 W^{3}Techs 的最新数据显示，截至 2024 年 2 月 19 日，在全球所有网站中，英文内容占 51.2%，其次是西班牙语（5.6%）、德语（5.0%）、日语（4.5%）、俄语（4.4%）、法语（4.3%），而中文内容仅占 1.3%。[1]（注：统计数据实时更新，但中文比例基本不变）由此可见，基于大语言模型的 ChatGPT 在自主训练过程中使用的语料大部分是英文。相对而言，ChatGPT 目前在英文上的表现优于其他语种。2023 年 3 月 14 日，微软官方网站发布声明，确认新版必应搜索引擎（New Bing）嵌入 GPT-4，实现了 Bing 与 ChatGPT 的深度融合。2023 年 3 月 21 日，谷歌推出与 ChatGPT、Bing GPT 抗衡的生成式人工智能产品 Google Bard。

---

[1] https://w3techs.com/technologies/overview/content_language

随着生成式人工智能表现越来越出色，人工翻译在惊讶之余不禁担忧：人工译者在多大程度上会被人工智能取代？具体到中国时政文本，以 ChatGPT 为代表的生成式人工智能表现如何？

与日常话语相比，时政话语有其鲜明特色。瑞典汉学家沈迈克指出，与日常话语相比，时政话语在句法、词汇、修辞手法等方面受到的限制更多 (*Five Essays on Chinese Political Words and Conduct*)。

笔者结合时政话语英译实践以及对 ChatGPT 等生成式人工智能的实验，从句法、词汇、修辞手法三个方面分享 ChatGPT 在中国时政话语英译中的表现。

4.1.1 句法

笔者在第二章详谈中英文在句法层面的差异。英文重"形合"，句子各部分离不开"and""but""however"等起承转合词连接。相反，"意合句"在中文时政文本中可谓比比皆是。推敲句子逻辑关系，准确把握句子内涵，是英译时政文本的第一步，也是至关重要的一步。

鉴于中英文这一关键句法差异，ChatGPT 在处理句子脉络（主谓宾）完整清晰、逻辑关系明确的中文文本时，较容易产出正确译文。试举两例：

我们要加强滥用行政权力排除、限制竞争执法。（国新办"激发市场活力 夯实高质量发展基础"主题发布会，2023-4-13）

人工译文：We will take stronger actions to exclude abuse of administrative power and restrict competitive law enforcement.

ChatGPT 译文：We need to strengthen law enforcement against abuse of administrative power to exclude and restrict competition.

译者未正确理解句子结构，把"滥用行政权力排除、限制竞争"误解为"排除滥用行政权力"与"限制（竞争）执法"并列，导致译文文理错乱，严重偏离原文。反观 ChatGPT，准确抓住了句子主干"我们要加强……执法"，准确识别了"执法"对象"滥用行政权力排除、限制竞争"。再看一个例子：

麦卡锡众议长无视国际社会对一个中国原则的广泛支持，无视"前车之鉴"，执意打"台湾牌"，无疑将重蹈覆辙，进一步损害中美关系，只会更加坚定中国人民同仇敌忾、支持国家统一的坚强意志和决心。（洛杉矶总领馆，2023–3–4）

人工译文：If Speaker McCarthy ignores the international community's broad support for the one-China principle, refuses to draw lessons from others' mistakes, and insists on playing the "Taiwan card", it will undoubtedly further damage China-US relations, and even strengthen the strong determination of the Chinese people to unite and fight for national reunification.

ChatGPT 译文：Speaker McCarthy ignores the widespread support of the international community for the One-China principle and disregards the lessons of history by insisting on playing the 'Taiwan card.' This will undoubtedly repeat past mistakes and further damage Sino-US relations. It will only strengthen the strong will and determination of the Chinese people to unite against a common enemy and support national unification.

对比两个版本的译文，ChatGPT 除了在"国家统一"一词上犯了错误之外（应使用"reunification"），其他部分有不少可圈可点之处。

人工译文把"无视'前车之鉴'"译为"refuses to draw lessons from others' mistakes"，ChatGPT 用词更简洁有力——"disregards the lessons of history"；人工译文漏译"重蹈覆辙"，ChatGPT 将"重蹈覆辙"译出——"repeat past mistakes"。"只会更加坚定中国人民同仇敌忾"一句，人工译文错用语气词"even"，ChatGPT 则恰当地使用"only"传递原文语气。

然而，若句子结构不完整、逻辑关系隐晦不明，ChatGPT 初译效果往往不佳，需要高水平人工译者辨识谬误并修正。以党的二十大报告中的一句为例：

> 加强宪法实施和监督，健全保证宪法全面实施的制度体系，更好发挥宪法在治国理政中的重要作用，维护宪法权威。

人工译文: We will better implement the Constitution and conduct constitutional oversight, and we will improve the systems for ensuring full compliance with the Constitution, so as to give better play to the Constitution's important role in China's governance and uphold its authority.

原文前两个分句谈具体措施，后两个分句谈目的与结果，前者较实（加强……监督，健全……体系），后者较虚（发挥……作用，维护……权威），逻辑关系隐藏其中，需要译者仔细推敲。人工译文以"so as to"连接上下，点明逻辑关系。

ChatGPT 译文：Strengthen the implementation and supervision of the Constitution, improve the institutional system that guarantees the full implementation of the Constitution, better play the important role of the Constitution in governing the country and administering politics, and safeguard the authority of the Constitution.

ChatGPT 照字面顺译，各分句并列排布，未能体现原文逻辑关系。另外，ChatGPT 将"治国理政"一词照字面机械地处理为"governing the country and administering politics"，不如"China's governance"简洁。

类似上例这种逻辑关系隐晦的无主句，在中国时政话语中比比皆是。再看一例：

加快完善公平竞争审查制度，推动制定公平竞争审查条例，健全公平竞争审查第三方评估、常态化抽查督查等机制制度。（国新办"激发市场活力 夯实高质量发展基础"主题发布会，2023–4–13）

ChatGP 译文：Accelerate the improvement of the fair competition review system, promote the formulation of fair competition review regulations, and improve the mechanisms and systems for third-party evaluation, regular spot checks and supervision of fair competition reviews.

经推敲分析，"制定条例""第三方评估""常态化抽查督查"都是比较实在的举措，是"完善……制度"的具体内容。ChatGPT 译文未能把握原文逻辑关系，且"fair competition review"在译文中重复堆叠，读来笨重拗口，显然有进一步完善的空间。

人工修改译文：We will move faster to improve the fair competition review system by promoting the formulation of regulations and enhancing third-party evaluation mechanisms. Regular spot checks and inspections will also be conducted.

修改后，以介词"by"承上启下，逻辑关系立时明晰，后文亦不必堆叠"fair competition review"，"常态化抽查督查"单独成句。把译文分成两句，一长一短，相互烘托，读来更清晰明快。

大量的实践证明，中文句法的"意合性"不但常常令人工译者"马失前蹄"，也是以 ChatGPT 为代表的生成式人工智能翻译路上的"绊脚石"。无论是对中文原文进行"译前编辑"，还是对译文进行"译后编辑"，都离不开高水平的人工译者积极干预，才能确保译文质量。

4.1.2 词汇

除了句法的"意合性"，时政文本中大量的中国特色词汇也是 ChatGPT 难以跨越的难关。比如，党的二十大报告中提到"不信邪、不怕鬼、不怕压"。"不怕鬼"这一形象表述进入时政话语，有特定的历史渊源，喻指中国人民克服内外压力的决心，绝不能像 ChatGPT 那样直译为"not be afraid of ghosts"。

理解中国特色表述，时政话语英译工作者不但要有足够的知识储备，要有"功夫在诗外"的学习意识，还要具备一定的政治素养。正如上一小节中所示，ChatGPT 把"国家统一"错译为"national unification"，不符合官方立场。台湾自古以来就是中国领土，是中国不可分割的一部分。我们要实现的是祖国再统一，"统一"应译为"reunification"，而不仅仅是大陆与台湾的简单合并（unification）。路透社注意到中国官方在"统一"一词译法上的谨慎，指出："台独"势力不太喜欢"reunification"一词，而是倾向于用"unification"。

同样，在处理"中国大陆"这一表述时，为避免掉入"两个中国"的话语陷阱，我们一贯使用"the mainland of China""China's mainland"或者"the Chinese mainland"，规避使用"mainland China"。当"民主党派"与中国共产党并列提及时，一般译为"other political parties"，单独出现时，可译为"non-CPC parties"（《中国时政话语翻译基本规范·英文》）。但是，ChatGPT 等人工智能并无此"政治意识"，一律将"民主党派"译为"democratic parties"，这既是机器直译的惯性，也是受现有英文语料影响的结果。

ChatGPT 训练的语料大部分是英文内容，其生成的内容自然不可避免地带有英文世界的话语习惯和意识形态色彩。比如，外媒常常把"China"与"Hong Kong"并列而提：

It generated $5.2 billion of revenue from China and Hong Kong last year, about 16% of its total revenue, according to Jefferies. (Reuters, May 22, 2023)

BBC 文章甚至称中国与香港之间存在"外交关系"：

Diplomatic relationship between Hong Kong and China has been on edge since 2019. (BBC, May 24, 2023)

近年来，欧美英文媒体、政府官员在提到"中国"时，频繁以"PRC (the People's Republic of China)"替代"China"，这一话语现象值得重视。虽然"PRC"与"China"都可指代"中国"，有些语境下可以互换，但二者侧重点不同。不妨听听 ChatGPT 对这一话语现象的看法。

问：It seems that American officials use "PRC" more frequently instead of just saying "China". Any comment?

ChatGPT: This is often done to distinguish between the government and political system of the People's Republic of China and the broader concept of "China" as a geographic and cultural entity.

西方媒体、政客刻意使用"PRC"替代"China"，刻意凸显"政治制度""政权"这一维度，是在刻意避开"China"这一更广博的国家概念。若再考虑"Taiwan"因素，西方政客吝于直接使用"China"一词描述"中国"，目的就更不单纯了。

国际传播工作者要懂语言现象背后的话语和政治逻辑，避免吃哑巴亏。英译中国时政话语，若盲信盲从人工智能生产的译文，很容易陷入西方话语陷阱，错而不自知。

ChatGPT 在翻译中国特色词汇方面有诸多局限，但并非毫无用武之地。高水平译者可以充分发挥它的交互式对话能力，获得翻译灵感。

2023 年 7 月 1 日起正式施行的《中华人民共和国对外关系法》中 8 次提到"基本"二字，官方发布的英文版中有 7 次用"fundamental"而非"basic"来翻译。比如：

坚持对外开放<u>基本国策</u>

adhere to the <u>fundamental policy</u> of opening to the outside world

"fundamental"与"basic"有何区别？用"fundamental"是否更能揭示政策与原则的重要性？

笔者求教 ChatGPT：Does "fundamental" add more shade of importance than "basic"?

> ChatGPT: The terms "fundamental" and "basic" often depend on context, <u>but in general, "fundamental" implies a deeper level of importance or significance compared to "basic."</u> Fundamentals are essential and foundational principles, while basics are simple, introductory concepts. <u>So, yes, "fundamental" does add more shade of importance than "basic."</u>

此例说明，善用生成式人工智能进行近义词辨析，与传统的检索方式相比可谓事半功倍。

会与 ChatGPT"聊天"，可以帮助译者准确理解原文，进而译对译准。比如，把"extremely unlikely"一词按照字面顺序译成"极不可能"对不对？不妨问问 ChatGPT。

问：Is "extremely unlikely" the same as "impossible"？

ChatGPT: "Extremely unlikely" suggests that the probability of an event occurring is very small or highly improbable, but not completely impossible. On the other hand, "impossible" refers to something that cannot occur or be done under any circumstances. It indicates that the event or outcome is not feasible or cannot happen in any conceivable way.

In summary, "extremely unlikely" implies an extremely low probability but still leaves a tiny chance for the event to happen, while "impossible" denotes an absolute impossibility with no possibility of occurrence.

由此可见，"extremely unlikely"指的是"可能性极小"，即，事件仍有发生的可能，若译成"极不可能"给中文读者的感觉是"可能性为零"，并不妥当。

在中英互译实践中，译者可以借助 ChatGPT 等生成式人工智能的交互能力，精准发问，反复发问，获取翻译灵感。这十分考验人工译者用英文提问的水平。

4.1.3 修辞手法

中国时政话语修辞手法丰富多样，包括排比、隐喻、明喻、用典、夸张等，以隐喻修辞最为突出。

ChatGPT 在识别英文隐喻、用典、夸张等修辞手法方面却独具"慧眼"。比如，让 ChatGPT 去辨识"江山就是人民，人民就是江山"英译文里的修辞手法：

问：The country is its people; the people are the country. Is this sentence metaphorically structured?

ChatGPT: Yes, the sentence "The country is its people; the people are the country" is structured metaphorically. It uses a metaphor to convey the idea that the essence of a country is its people and that the people are what make up the country. The sentence equates two things (the country and its people) to emphasize their close relationship and interdependence.

"江山就是人民，人民就是江山"是独具中国特色的政治宣言。英译这种结构对称、表达凝练、内涵丰富的特色政治表达，要兼顾内涵与形式。英译"江山就是人民，人民就是江山"这句隐喻表达，直译就是最好的译法。把形式打散，让译文看不到一点原文的"形"，并非上策。ChatGPT尚能识别译文的隐喻修辞，人工译者更应懂得欣赏。有句英文经典论断与之形似。美国司法史上有一经典案例——联合公民（Citizens United）诉联邦选举委员会（Federal Election Commission）案，美国最高法院的最终判决认为，联邦法律限制企业资助候选人的相关条款违宪。判决发布后，美国媒体围绕"Corporations are people; money is speech.（企业就是人；金钱就是言论。）"这一论断展开激烈争论，十分热闹。"Corporations are people; money is speech."也是隐喻表达，寥寥数语表达"企业也和人一样拥有言论自由，企业资助候选人本质上是在表达言论"。

时政文本中常见的隐喻包括"战争隐喻""天气隐喻""动物隐喻"等。实践观察发现，ChatGPT在处理时政话语中的隐喻表达时，倾向于采取"直译"法，即，保留原文中的隐喻意象。这一倾向使得ChatGPT在翻译隐喻表达时表现很不稳定，常常需要经验丰富的人工译者把关。试举一例：

> 使党始终成为风雨来袭时全体人民最可靠的主心骨。（党的二十大报告）

ChatGPT 译文：(This will) make the Party always <u>the most reliable backbone</u> of all the people when storms come.

人工译文：This will ensure that our Party always remains <u>the pillar</u> that the Chinese people can <u>lean on</u> in times of difficulty.

ChatGPT 以"storms"译"风雨"，将"最可靠的主心骨"直译为"the most reliable backbone"，保留了原文的隐喻意象。但是，这样的译文是经不起考验的。首先，以最高级"the most reliable"修饰"backbone"，使人感觉还有"other less reliable backbones"，而"backbone"只有一个。因此，"the most reliable backbone"虽然与原文形似，但英文读来有些奇怪。其次，短短一句话中存在两个迥异的隐喻意象（"backbone"与"storms"），构成"混合隐喻（mixed metaphor）"（参考本书第二章），极易给英文读者制造阅读困惑。

对比来看，人工译文舍弃"风雨"画面，译成直白明了的英文"in times of difficulty"，并以"pillar（支柱）"替换"主心骨"，避免使用"the most reliable backbone"这种奇怪表述，也避免了在一句话中出现"混合隐喻"。整句译文自然流畅且直白易懂。

英译隐喻表达，要特别注意避免"隐喻误解（metaphorical misunderstanding）"，即，把原文中的隐喻意象直译到英文中，可能引起理解偏差，甚至严重误解。以 ChatGPT 为代表的生成式人工智能在规避隐喻误解方面远不如人工译者思考周密。这方面案例很多，比如：

谁妄想这样干，必将在 14 亿多中国人民用血肉铸成的钢铁长城面前碰得头破血流！（习近平总书记在庆祝中国共产党成立 100 周年大会上的讲话）

人工译文：Anyone who would attempt to do so will find themselves on a collision course with a Great Wall of steel forged by over 1.4 billion Chinese people.

ChatGPT 译文：Those who dare to do so will undoubtedly meet a bloody end before the Great Wall of steel and flesh constructed by over 1.4 billion Chinese people!

ChatGPT 译文保留了原文中的隐喻意象，极易造成隐喻误解。中国人说"血肉铸成的钢铁长城"，是在表达捍卫国家的坚强决心，而非要在人们脑海中勾勒出一幅"血肉"与"钢铁"浇铸而成的长城画面。人工译文舍弃"血肉"，只保留"钢铁"（a Great Wall of steel），没有硬贴原文，是得体的译法，而 ChatGPT 译文"the Great Wall of steel and flesh"营造的画面有些血腥。

关于"头破血流"四个字，部分外媒在翻译时极力渲染"血腥"画面，比如，《纽约时报》将其翻译为"crack their heads and spill blood"。这种翻译策略，貌似忠实原文，实际上是以血腥画面吸引流量并刻意迎合对华偏见。

翻译"头破血流"这四个字，译者首先要回答一个问题："头破血流"是在表达捍卫国家的决心，还是刻意制造血腥画面？当我们说"某人非得碰得头破血流才肯回头"，是要渲染血腥画面还是在强调某人的倔脾气？对懂中文的读者而言，答案似乎是显而易见的。因此，把"头破血流"直译成"血淋淋（bloody）"的画面，是以"伪忠实"刻意渲染血腥暴力，本末倒置，损伤国家形象。

英译时政话语里的隐喻表达，隐喻意象是去是留，抑或是替换，需要经验丰富的译者根据具体情况权衡分析。译者要洞察中英文语言表达习惯差异以及隐喻思维方式差异，避免以"伪忠实"制造隐喻误解。这种权衡与思考，是 ChatGPT 等生成式人工智能目前尚无法独立完成的。

英译中国时政话语，以 ChatGPT 为代表的生成式人工智能虽有不少可圈可点之处，但在句法、词汇、修辞手法等方面依然面临不少"拦路虎"，需要经验丰富的高水平人工译者介入。国家层面的时政话语英译，不单单是文字的简单转换，还要考虑政治立场、话语竞争、国家形象等多重因素。

人工智能带来的翻译恐慌，不应该是职业恐慌，而应是本领恐慌。

周恩来总理曾这样告诫翻译工作者："搞翻译不是那么简单的，不是懂几句外国话就行的。不但要有政治水平，同时要有较高的文化水平。没有基本功和丰富的知识不行。基本功包括三个方面：政治思想、语言本身和各种文化知识。"（《周恩来选集》）面对人工智能，时政话语英译工作者不必轻言"取代"，更务实的态度是，让大语言模型赋能翻译学习，夯实译者基本功，丰富译者知识储备，让人工智能成为辅助人工翻译的利器。

4.2 ChatGPT 赋能翻译学习

利用好大语言模型在英文语料方面得天独厚的优势，赋能英文学习，是广大翻译工作者亟须掌握的技能。笔者结合阅读英文文学作品的经历，分享 ChatGPT 的几则妙用，供读者举一反三。

美国作家赛珍珠（Pearl S. Buck）的经典小说《大地》（*The Good Earth*）第十三章这样描述"声音"：

Then out of the dusk there answered him a voice, a deep burly voice.

权威英文词典告诉我们，形容词"burly"一般只有"（身材）强壮魁梧"之意。比如：

(adjective) describes a man who is large and strong（《剑桥高级学习词典》）

A burly man has a broad body and strong muscles.（《柯林斯高级英语学习词典》）

作家用词往往不落俗套，富于想象力，以"burly"修饰声音，显然是隐喻用法。如何隐喻，用法是否得体？读者身边若无学养深厚的英文专家，不妨求助 ChatGPT。

要善于用英文向 ChatGPT 发问，提问得越贴切，生成的答案也越贴切。

问：Is it correct to use "burly" to describe voice?

ChatGPT: While "burly" is typically used to describe a person's physical appearance, it can be used metaphorically to describe a voice in certain contexts. In this usage, it suggests a deep, powerful, and resonant quality to the voice. However, it's important to note that "burly" is not commonly used to describe voices, so it may sound unusual or out of place to some readers or listeners. Alternative words like "deep," "rich," or "sonorous" are more commonly used to describe voices.

ChatGPT 告诉我们，以"burly"修饰声音虽然并非常见用法，但亦可接受，属于作家的创造性发挥。以身材的"魁梧健壮"喻声音的"雄健浑厚（deep and powerful）"，使文字更生动、更富创造性。ChatGPT 在回答中还推荐了"deep""rich""sonorous"等同义词。

赛珍珠或许是受"stout"一词的启发。"stout"最常用的意思也是"（身材）粗壮结实"，但在文学作品中还可表达"resolute/determined"之意。

(literary) strong and determined（《剑桥高级学习词典》）

小说中，主人公王龙带着妻儿老小逃饥荒，老婆阿兰说可以把小女儿卖掉，好凑钱早日回归家园。但是，王龙坚决不同意。王龙坚定地说：

"Never would I," said Wang Lung stoutly, "not though I spent my life in this wilderness."

把这句话输入 ChatGPT，它准确给出"stoutly"在具体语境下的内涵：

In the given context, the word "stoutly" is used to describe how Wang Lung spoke, indicating that he spoke in a resolute, determined, and firm manner. It implies that he spoke with conviction and strength, emphasizing his unwavering stance on the matter being discussed.

由这两个修饰词联想到钱锺书先生谈"笑声"的一段趣论：

西洋成语称笑声清扬者为"银笑"，假幽默像掺了铅的伪币，发出重浊呆木的声音，只能算铅笑。不过，"银笑"也许是卖笑得利，笑中有银之意，好比说"书中有黄金屋"；姑备一说，供给辞典学者的参考。(《写在人生边上》)

英文"silvery laugh（银笑）"是隐喻表达，抛开钱先生的幽默趣解，我们不妨思考一下：以"silvery"修饰声音，源自何处？

笔者请教英文外专也未获答案。不妨再次发挥大语言模型的作用，接着 ChatGPT 对"stoutly"那段阐释追问：Just like "silvery" in "silvery laugh"？

ChatGPT: Yes, just like "stoutly" in the previous example, "silvery" can also be used metaphorically to describe a laugh. When used in this way, "silvery" suggests that the laugh is light, clear, and musical in tone, much like the sound of a silver bell. It is not being used to describe the physical appearance of the person laughing, but rather the quality of their laughter.

答案中的"much like the sound of a silver bell"为我们揭开迷雾。"silver table bell"曾是西方上流社会的专属，银铃一响，仆人就可以上菜了。用价值昂贵的银来打制铃铛，也是财富与地位的象征。

从这句"'silvery' suggests that the laugh is light, clear, and musical in tone"来看，钱先生把"silvery laugh"译成"笑声清扬"是多么贴切！

勤读英文原著，是译者锤炼语言基本功的必由之路。翻译学习者不妨把以 ChatGPT 为代表的生成式人工智能工具视为可以随时求助的外籍专家，勤于发问，善于发问，让它们成为解决英文"疑难杂症"、辅助翻译学习的"神兵利器"。

在工作实践中，笔者时不时会与 ChatGPT、Bing GPT、Google Bard 等生成式人工智能工具"聊聊天"，既能获取语言灵感，又能诊断诸多"疑难杂症"。前外交部翻译室主任陈明明大使把以 ChatGPT 为代表的生成式人工智能工具戏称为"聊天狗"。与"聊天狗"互动，很考验提问者的"投喂"能力。换言之，问题越精准，"聊天狗"吐出的答案也越贴切。

4.2.1 识别用典、夸张等修辞手法

《经济学人》文章谈及国际经济体系，文中有一处用典修辞，挺有创意。笔者将文字投喂给"聊天狗"，问：

"The way that we are going to build an international economic architecture is not going to be with Parthenon-style clear pillars as we did after the end of the Second World

War, but something that feels a little bit more like Frank Gehry." (*The Economist*, May 16, 2023) What figure of speech is used in "Parthenon-style" and "Frank Gehry"?

帕特农神庙与解构主义建筑大师弗兰克·盖里（Frank O. Gehry）在西方社会广为人知。《经济学人》文章谈国际经济体系，引用这两个元素作对比，旨在表达什么？请看 Bing GPT 的回答。

> Bing GPT: In your example, "Parthenon-style" and "Frank Gehry" are both <u>allusions</u>, which are a type of figure of speech that refer to something well-known or famous.
>
> The Parthenon is an ancient Greek temple that is famous for its classical architecture and <u>symmetry</u>. Frank Gehry is a modern architect who is known for his <u>unconventional and innovative designs</u>. <u>By contrasting these two allusions, the speaker implies that the international economic architecture will be more complex and dynamic than the previous one.</u>

帕特农神庙柱式比例和谐，布局平衡对称，是古希腊建筑的典范；而当代著名解构主义建筑大师弗兰克·盖里则以设计奇特不规则著称，恰恰与帕特农神庙的建筑风格相反。二者的建筑风格形成鲜明对比，借此说明当今的国际经济体系要比二战后更复杂、更多变。用典的妙处就在于，借助同一文化里广为人知的符号，起到"一句顶一万句"的功效。

笔者在第二章"夸张的误用"一节提及 BBC 报道中的一句夸张表述：But I'm not important enough as a college student with eight cents to my name.

问：Is this a hyperbolic expression?

Bing GPT: Yes, the statement can be seen as a hyperbolic expression. The person is emphasizing their financial situation by stating they only have eight cents to their name, and <u>implying that this lack of money makes them unimportant.</u>

4.2.2 识别谐音梗

问：We are going to hold a forum on the Greater Bay Area in China ("大湾区" in Chinese). Does the theme "湾-derful Future: Fusion and Connection" make sense to you?

Bing GPT: Yes, the title "湾derful Future: Fusion and Connection" makes sense to me. <u>It's a play on words with "湾" (Bay) and "wonderful"</u>, and it also includes the themes of fusion and connection which could be relevant to the Greater Bay Area in China.

《经济学人》报道印度假发产业，文章结尾玩了一个谐音梗。请看：

Clamping down on smuggling is understandable. But it is legitimate traders who are having toupee. (*The Economist*, November 3, 2022)

问：What does "having toupee" mean?

Bing GPT: The phrase "having toupee" is a pun on the word "toupée", which is a small wig or artificial hairpiece worn to cover a bald spot. <u>The pun plays on the homophony between "toupée" and "to pay"</u>, implying that the legitimate traders are suffering the costs of the smuggling crackdown. *The Economist* often uses puns and wordplay in its headlines and articles to add humor and wit to its reporting. Do you enjoy reading *The Economist*?

它不但轻松识破"having toupee"与"having to pay"的谐音梗,还指出《经济学人》喜欢在标题和文章中玩文字游戏。真是一只火眼金睛且见多识广的"聊天狗"!

4.2.3 破解语言"疑难杂症"

中国时政话语英译要注意很多细节,小到一个介词、一个不定冠词都可能蕴含特殊政治意义。笔者用英文问:

In the phrase "Xi Jinping Thought on Socialism with Chinese Characteristics for a New Era", why is the preposition "for" used instead of "in"? ("习近平新时代中国特色社会主义思想"英文译法为何用介词"for"而不用"in"?)

Bing GPT: The preposition "for" is used in the phrase "Xi Jinping Thought on Socialism with Chinese Characteristics for a New Era" to indicate that <u>the thought is intended to guide or shape the new era. The use of "for" implies purpose or intention, whereas "in" would simply indicate a time frame or location</u>. In this context, "for" is used to convey that the thought is meant to have an active role in shaping the future.

用介词"for"而不用"in",意在体现主观上的"能动性",体现"新思想"与"新时代"之间的关系,Bing GPT 的回答可谓言简意赅。

无论是读英文书还是读外媒,遇到语言"疑难杂症",不妨与"聊天狗"互动一下,不断改进"投喂"技巧,让它成为辅助英文学习的神器。笔者读《经济学人》遇到一段文字,针对其中的一处形象用词"swoosh"发问。请看:

"Adidas's market value is back down to €25bn, one-seventh that of Nike. Investors today appear to have more confidence not just in the swoosh but in Puma, Adidas's smaller domestic rival." (*The Economist*, March 23, 2023) Why is "swoosh" used here instead of Nike?

Bing GPT: In this context, the word "swoosh" is used as a metonym for Nike. A metonym is a figure of speech in which a thing or concept is referred to by the name of something closely associated with it. In this case, the "swoosh" is closely associated with Nike because it is the company's logo. The writer may have chosen to use "swoosh" instead of "Nike" to add variety to their writing to create a more informal tone.

Bing GPT 不但告诉我们"swoosh"是耐克的商标,而且还指出了转喻(metonym)修辞手法。另外,用"swoosh"也避免重复使用"Nike"一词,是新闻写作用词多样化的体现。

问:Lockhart R.H. *Memoirs of a British Agent*. London, [1935], between p. 230-231 (facs.). What does "facs." mean?

Bing GPT: <u>Facs. is an abbreviation that stands for facsimile or facsimile edition</u>. It means that the book is <u>a reproduction of the original edition</u>, usually by photographic means. It is often used in bibliographies to indicate the source of a quotation or reference.

4.2.4 根据风格要求润色文字

Bing GPT 在润色社交媒体推文方面有着不俗的表现。

问：Rewrite this tweet to make it more colorful：""It's tulip time! About 220,000 tulips of 25 varieties are blooming at the gorgeous Renmin park in Qinghai Province, northwest China. This colorful sea of flowers has attracted flocks of tourists."" (Xinhua, May 6, 2023)

Bing GPT: <u>Here is a more colorful version of the tweet:</u> "Tulip <u>mania</u> has hit Renmin Park in Qinghai Province, northwest China! A <u>stunning</u> display of 220,000 tulips in 25 vibrant varieties has created a <u>breathtaking</u> sea of color. Tourists are flocking to witness this <u>floral extravaganza</u>!"

可以看出，为了实现"让推文更有色彩"这一要求，Bing GPT 在选词上朝着辞藻华丽、吸引眼球这个方向努力，比如"mania""stunning""breathtaking""extravaganza"。

笔者调整要求，变换任务，问：Rewrite this tweet to make it more literary (sound like Shakespeare).

> Bing GPT: Here is a more literary version of the tweet that sounds like Shakespeare: Hark! The time of tulips doth arrive. In fair Renmin park of Qinghai Province, a wonderous sight to see: two hundred and twenty thousand blooms of five and twenty kinds. A sea of color, drawing crowds from near and far.

Bing GPT 在三秒内完成了这一任务，选词用词（如"hark""doth""fair""wonderous""from near and far"）朝着增加文学性和用词"做旧"的方向努力，表现十分惊艳。未来，"聊天狗"会不断成长成熟，对翻译和国际传播工作者而言，这既是挑战也是机遇。在人工智能面前，人不能"躺平"，反而应越发追求精进。ChatGPT 等生成式人工智能工具在翻译和英文写作方面的确有可圈可点之处，但错误和滑稽之处也不少。如果人的水平跟不上节奏，很容易被机器忽悠而不自知。

ChatGPT 似乎对自己的翻译水平有自知之明，时不时地在译文后加一句备注：

> Note: This is a rough translation, as the original sentence may have more nuanced meaning and context that could affect the translation.

实践证明，正是文字中那只可意会却难以言传的"nuance"，是人工智能尚无法完全取代专业人工翻译的关键所在。佛家把众生称之为"有情（sentient beings）"，世间的文字多半也注入了有情众生的心识与情感，因而，有很大一部分的文字工作是需要有情的人去感知文字的冷暖，感知文字的细微之处。这既是翻译、写作等文字工作的乐趣，也是熬人心神的地方。

4.3 ChatGPT 与公示语翻译

笔者在北京朝阳公园见到一块提示牌，上书中英双语提示语：

全园禁止烟火
No naked lights

英译文对不对？不妨问问 ChatGPT：Does this sentence make sense：No naked lights?

ChatGPT: Yes, the sentence "No naked lights" makes sense. It is a straightforward instruction or warning indicating that the use of an open flame or exposed light source (a "naked light") is not allowed or should be avoided in a particular context. This phrase is often used in situations where there may be flammable materials or potentially hazardous conditions.

"No naked lights"是正确译法。ChatGPT 轻松判定这句英文标语是否地道，并给出详细解释。

笔者在自家小区偶见一块提示牌，英译文明显错误。请看：

禁止高空坠物
Don't throw at upper air

介词"at"最滑稽，"throw at upper air"成了"向高空扔东西"，与原文意思反了。怎么改？不妨与 ChatGPT 聊聊天。请看聊天记录：

问：Don't throw at upper air. Is this proper English?

ChatGPT: The phrase "Don't throw at upper air" is not considered proper English. It seems to be a combination of words that doesn't form a coherent sentence.

接着告诉它：It's a clumsy translation of 禁止高空坠物.

ChatGPT: Ah, I see! In that case, the phrase "<u>Don't throw objects from high places</u>" would be a more appropriate translation of 禁止高空坠物. It conveys the meaning more clearly in English.

还可以继续向它提要求，比如，把译文缩短、改变语气语调等。人工译者不一定要对 ChatGPT 言听计从，但与其聊天可以获得不少灵感。

受此启发，笔者每次在公共场所看到公示语奇葩译文便忍不住与 ChatGPT 聊聊天，不聊出满意译文不罢休。笔者在西宁机场卫生间洗手台看到：

感应出水

Induction of water

英译文看上去像是从某个机器翻译平台直译过来的，译得一塌糊涂，不知所云。如何修改？请看笔者与 ChatGPT 的聊天记录：

问：What does this mean: Induction of water?

ChatGPT: The phrase "induction of water" is not a standard English expression, and its meaning is not immediately clear without further context. It could be a technical term used in a specific field or domain. If you can provide more context or clarify the context in which you encountered this phrase, I'd be happy to try and help you understand its meaning better.

ChatGPT 指出"induction of water"并非标准英文，在没有更详细语境的情况下，它也不知道其所指何物。笔者接着问：

Lol~It's an awkward translation of 感应出水 (meaning automatic faucet).

ChatGPT: Ah, I see! That makes sense now. "Induction of water" is indeed an awkward translation of 感应出水, which means "automatic faucet" in English. Automatic faucets are designed to turn on and off without the need for manual operation. They use sensors or proximity detectors to detect the presence of hangs or objects and activate the water flow accordingly. These faucets are commonly found in public restrooms and other facilities to promote water conservation and hygiene.

与"automatic faucet"类似的表达还有"hands-free faucet""touchless faucet"等，都是一目了然的英文表达。在这个案例中，笔者脑海中有比较成熟的译文，拿 ChatGPT 来验证，人机双管齐下，很快确定正确译文。

当然，译者脑中若无成熟初译也无妨，只需与 ChatGPT 多聊几个回合。以常令人工译者头疼的"文明"二字为例。在党的二十大报告中，"文明"二字出现数十次，只有在表达广义的文明状态时才译成"civilization"，其他情况下都不宜照字面直译。比如：

尊重世界<u>文明</u>多样性

respect the diversity of <u>civilizations</u>

中华<u>文明</u>的智慧结晶

the crystallization of the wisdom of Chinese <u>civilization</u>

大力推进<u>生态文明建设</u>

We have made a big push to enhance <u>ecological conservation</u>.

坚定不移走生产发展、生活富裕、生态良好的<u>文明发展道路</u>。

We will continue to pursue a model of <u>sound development</u> featuring improved production, higher living standards, and healthy ecosystems.

可见，"文明"二字使用的场景极其广泛，也具有鲜明的"意会性"和"非确指性"。当"文明"二字进入公示语，又常常令译者大伤脑筋。比如，如何翻译"请文明养狗"，请看笔者与"聊天狗"的一番对话。

先提一个请求并问一个问题：Explain 请文明养狗 in English. Is there any equivalent expression in English?

第四章　ChatGPT：机遇与挑战 | 195

Bing GPT: 请文明养狗 is a Chinese phrase that means "please raise a dog civilly" or "please keep dogs with civilization". <u>It is a slogan that encourages dog owners to be responsible and considerate of others when they have pets.</u> Some of the common rules of <u>civil dog raising</u> are:

1. Keep the dog on a leash and muzzle when walking outside.

2. Clean up the dog's poop and dispose of it properly.

3. Give the dog regular vaccinations and health checks.

4. Register the dog with the authorities and get a license.

5. Avoid disturbing the neighbors with the dog's barking or running.

I don't think there is an exact equivalent expression in English, but some possible ways to convey the same idea are:

1. Be a responsible dog owner.

2. Respect others when you have a dog.

3. Follow the etiquette of dog keeping.

4. Keep your dog under control and clean.

Bing GPT 的这段回答，信息量很大，且"鱼龙混杂"。把"请文明养狗"直译成"please raise a dog civilly"或者"please keep dogs with civilization"显然是不可以的，但 Bing GPT 对"请文明养狗"的阐释是非常准确到位的，"responsible"一词尤其给人工译者灵感。笔者注意到"civil dog raising"这一表述，于是接着追问：civil dog raising?

Bing GPT: Yes, civil dog raising is a term that I made up to translate 文明养犬, which is the noun form of 请文明养狗. It means to raise a dog in a way that respects the rights and feelings of other people and animals. Do you have a dog or are you interested in getting one?

问：Is this phrase commonly used in English?

Bing GPT: No, it is not a common phrase in English. I just created it as a possible translation of the Chinese phrase. A more common way to say it in English would be "be a responsible dog owner" or "follow the etiquette of dog keeping".

至此，答案已经出来了。此处的"文明"二字较恰当的译法是"responsible"。"请文明养狗"不妨译为"Be a responsible dog owner."。国际动物保护组织"Four Paws International"在其官网呼吁宠物爱好者要"当文明养宠人（Be a responsible pet owner.）"，并具体列举了宠物主人应尽的四大责任，其中就包括"养狗要拴绳""及时清理排泄物"等社会责任。

以 ChatGPT 为代表的人工智能工具好比英文知识储备丰富但中文水平有待提高的语言专家，更妙的是，它不会厌烦，且随时待命。但要记住一点，提问者也必须具备一定的语言功底，才能做到有效发问，识别答案中的亮点与谬误，从中获取灵感。

4.4 活用 ChatGPT 辨析同义词

笔者在《笔尖上的文化碰撞：对外话语与翻译》一书中提醒广大英文学习者要多查英英词典，不要被英汉词典给出的中文释义"困住脑袋"。如果对单词的认识流于片面，到实践应用中可能会故步自封甚至笑话百出。勤查英英词典有助于更好地进行同义词辨析。

然而，以 ChatGPT 为代表的生成式人工智能工具问世以来，笔者的这条建议就显得有些落伍了。随着新技术的出现，借助英英词典辨析同义词不再是首选，因为活用 ChatGPT 可以事半功倍。

本书第一章"用词"一节谈到同义词之间的"词气"有微妙差异。外媒编辑部在选词用词上有"具体、形象"的考量，常常要在同义词之间斟酌，因此勤读外媒是细致把握同义词微妙差异的法门。如果读者具备一定的词语储备和语言敏感性，在生成式人工智能的帮助下，可以获得一份全新的阅读体验。

《经济学人》报道合肥市政府大力"投资"高科技企业，动词"plough"用得很形象：

> While cities elsewhere in the world fund schools, build sewers or house the poor, Hefei's administration ploughs money into the most promising companies it can identify. (*The Economist*, August 5, 2023)

动词"plough"意思是"犁地"，用在投资语境显然是隐喻用法。那么，我们不妨问一问 Bing GPT：为什么不用更平实的动词

"invest"而用"plough"？

　　Bing GPT: The verb ploughs means to turn up the earth of an area of land with a plow, especially before sowing seed or planting. <u>It is often used as a metaphor to express the idea of putting a lot of effort, money, or resources into something, especially with the hope of getting a good return or result.</u> For example, you can say "He ploughed all his savings into his new business" or "She ploughed through the book in one night". The verb ploughs is used in this sentence to contrast Hefei's administration with other cities that fund schools, build sewers, or house the poor. <u>The verb ploughs also suggests that Hefei's administration is confident and ambitious in its strategy, and that it expects to reap the benefits of its investments in the future.</u> I hope this helps you understand why the verb ploughs is used in this sentence.

　　正如农民犁地必然期待好收成，"ploughs money into"不仅道出了"投资力度大"，也暗含"期待投资有好回报"。"plough"与"invest"相比，形象生动且言简义丰。Bing GPT不仅点出"plough"是隐喻用法，而且结合语境指出这个词与前句其他城市的做法形成对比。

　　有生成式人工智能这样随时待命的英文外专，我们读外媒是不是别有一番滋味？再看一例。

　　State media said that downpours in the mountains of Hebei had caused Hebei's Juma River to flood in Zhuozhou. A levee on the nearby Baigou River, into which the Juma River flows, <u>gave way</u> near Zhuozhou, forcing the evacuation of four villages. (*The New York Times*, August 4, 2023)

《纽约时报》报道河北水灾，描述决堤用动词短语"give way"，而非"break"或者"burst open"，为什么？请看聊天记录：

问：What does "gave way" mean in this context？

Bing GPT: In this sentence, gave way means to break or collapse <u>under pressure or force</u>. When the levee gave way, <u>it means that it could not withstand the water pressure from the river and it broke</u>, allowing the water to flow into the nearby villages. I hope this helps you understand the meaning of gave way in this context.

Bing GPT 对"give way"的解释与《剑桥高级学习词典》的释义一致：to break, especially when under pressure from strong forces，读者可放心采纳。

接着问：Why not just use broke?

Bing GPT: That's a good question. <u>The word broke</u> can also mean to split or burst open, <u>but it is more general and does not imply the cause or the result of the breaking</u>. For example, you can say "I broke the vase" or "The vase broke", but you don't know how or why it happened, or what happened afterwards. <u>The word give way is more specific and implies that something broke under pressure or force, and that it caused some consequences or changes</u>. For example, you can say "The levee gave way to the flood" or "The flood made the levee give way".

Bing GPT 指出"broke"一词较笼统，而"gave way"更"具体（specific）"，内涵更丰富，点出了决堤的原因——"under pressure or force"。Bing GPT 好似一位受过新闻写作专业训练的编辑，把选词用词的逻辑交代得明明白白。虽然"give way"与"break"在这个语境下并无实质区别，都可以用来表达决堤，写作实践中"the levee broke"也很常见，但"give way"承载的信息量更大。

实际上，Bing GPT 凭借强大的大语言模型，可抵千万个"资深编辑""资深外专"的知识储备，用它来辅助外媒阅读，总能有意外收获。笔者读《经济学人》，被一则标题吸引：

Italy's scorching summer <u>singes</u> Giorgia Meloni (*The Economist*, August 3, 2023)

动词"singe"用得妙极了。好在哪儿？还是听听 Bing GPT 老师如何回答。

问：Why *The Economist* uses "singes" in this headline?

Bing GPT: That's a good question. The word singes in this headline is a verb that means <u>to burn superficially or lightly</u>. *The Economist* uses this word as a metaphor to describe how the scorching summer in Italy has affected the popularity and performance of Giorgia Meloni, the prime minister of Italy since October 2022. <u>The word singes is a clever choice by the writer because it creates a vivid image and a contrast between</u>

the literal and figurative meanings of heat and fire. It also conveys a sense of urgency and drama, which can attract the reader's attention and curiosity.

标题中特意选用动词"singe",分寸拿捏得很到位。"singe"不似"burn"或者"sear"那般严重,指的是"burn superficially(表面燎一下)"。意大利总理焦尔吉娅·梅洛尼(Giorgia Meloni)面临一个窘境:投票支持她的选民中大部分人不相信气候变化,但民调显示,80%以上的意大利人认为气候变化的威胁是实实在在的。夏日的高温热浪令人们质疑梅洛尼政府的气候变化政策。因此,《经济学人》标题幽默地指出,"炎炎夏日燎到了梅洛尼"。"singe"是隐喻表达,很形象,正如 Bing GPT 所言,也吸引读者注意,勾起读者的好奇心。另外,"scorching summer singes"有明显的头韵构词考虑。

如果把"singe"替换为同义词"burn",标题给人怎样的感觉?

接着追问:Why not use burn?

Bing GPT: That's a good question. The word burn in this headline is also a possible choice, but it has a different connotation and effect than singe. The word burn implies a more severe and extensive action of burning, while the word singe implies a more mild and superficial action of burning.

Therefore, if *The Economist* used burn instead of singe in the headline, it would imply that Italy's scorching summer has burned Giorgia Meloni's popularity and performance more seriously and extensively, and that it caused more pain and harm to her and her government. This might not be the intended message or tone that the writer wanted to convey, as it might sound too exaggerated or sensational.

新闻写作要讲究选词的艺术。记者编辑要根据文章主旨拿捏好选词的"轻重"。当描述一件事情有多个备选词可用，对同义词"词气"的把握就显得特别关键。从编辑部视角读外媒，笔者看到"singe"便忍不住想："为何不用'burn'等同义词"？读罢全文再回眸，更觉标题选词分寸得当。这看似细枝末节的琐事，实则关乎新闻报道是否客观公正。

《纽约时报》曾在报道中用"toxic"一词描述奥巴马与教师联合会的紧张关系：

> In fact, Mr. Obama's ties with teachers' unions have grown increasingly toxic. (*The New York Times*, March 24, 2015)

《纽约时报》分管内容规范的副总编辑菲利普·科比特把这处用词当作反面案例警示编辑部：

> "Toxic," meaning poisonous, seems like an overstatement; "strained" may be closer to the mark. And once again we're mixing metaphors; as a colleague said, a "toxic tie" sounds like a weapon in a James Bond movie. (*The New York Times*, April 21, 2015)

科比特指出，用"有毒的"描述奥巴马与教师联合会的关系有些言过其词，不如"strained（紧张的）"更贴切。另外，"toxic tie"是混合隐喻，正如《纽约时报》一位编辑戏言，"a toxic tie"

听着像 007 系列电影中的武器。"tie（领带、绳、线）"与"toxic/poisonous"搭配不但有些夸张，还有些滑稽，不如"a strained tie"自然顺畅。

《纽约时报》专栏作家法哈德·曼朱（Farhad Manjoo）曾撰文分享 ChatGPT 如何深刻改变了自己的工作方式。法哈德列举了 ChatGPT 在辅助新闻写作方面的三大用处：（1）找词（Wordfinding）；（2）让写作不再卡壳（Getting unstuck）；（3）梳理总结信息（Summarizing）。

据报道，OpenAI 为了让 ChatGPT 的语言合成结果更自然流畅，用了 45TB 的数据、近 1 万亿个单词来训练模型，大概是 1351 万本牛津词典。[1] 如此惊人的词汇量，非人力所能匹敌。我们唯有主动拥抱新技术，让新技术成为辅助我们学习进步的良师益友。《纽约时报》记者借助 ChatGPT "找词"，我们读外媒不妨也活用 ChatGPT 辨析词语。如此既开卷有益，又开卷有趣。

---

[1] http://zj.news.cn/2023-02/21/c_1129382688.htm

后记

常常有读者在笔者的微信公号"外宣微记"留言，希望推荐翻译学习书籍。《论英汉翻译技巧》是每次必荐之书。这本书汇集了多位翻译前辈总结的翻译技巧，实用性和可读性极强。其中，翻译前辈张培基先生《论习语的汉译英》一文专谈习语（包括成语、俗语、谚语、歇后语等）英译，分析了中英习语的特点、习语的可译性、习语英译的两种形式主义偏向，并总结习语英译的九种方法。

学习翻译，首先要掌握翻译技巧，好比习武要习练招式。在此基础上，多实践、多阅读，在实践和阅读中再回头品味翻译技巧，感受中英文语言风格特点，久而久之必定收获良多。前辈名家早已把理论和技巧备足，我们更需要的是"从实践中来到实践中去"，多解决一些实际问题。

语言本身绝非独立王国，而是现实的反映。中英文语言外壳虽不一样，但在很多情况下，外壳背后的思维习惯是一样的。中国人说"小巫见大巫"，英文用"dwarf"一词表达足矣。"dwarf"作名词时表达"侏儒"之意，作动词时意思是：To cause to appear small by comparison（《美国传统词典》）。A dwarfs B：B 与 A 相比，小巫见大巫！

笔者读《经济学人》多次读到这样一句话：(He wanted) a bonfire of red tape. "bonfire"即"篝火"，"red tape"即"繁文缛节"或者"官僚作风"。把这句英文用中国成语译出来可以是：把繁文缛节付之一炬！反过来，把成语"付之一炬"译成英文就可以考虑"bonfire"这个词。

时政话语中经常出现成语、俗语等中国特色表达，我们首先要坚信特色表达的可译性。"可译性"主要指"主旨内涵"可译，而非要搞形式对等。能做到形神兼备当然最好，但切不可被语言外壳吓住，或不知所措，或走向逐字硬译的形式主义错误。中国网民创造了网络热词"雪糕刺客"，用来指"那些隐藏在冰柜里面，看着其貌不扬，但当你拿去付钱的时候会用它的价格刺你一下的雪糕"。英文竟然也有类似表达："The brand that Ambushed customers with a $400 clothespin."。中文叫"刺客"，英文也巧用"ambush（埋伏）"表达一样的意思，不谋而合，真是有趣。这是读外媒、品翻译之乐。

翻译学习没有捷径。掌握心法，广泛阅读积累，从实践中来到实践中去，就是唯一的途径。今天的移动互联网时代，我们的学习条件比当年的翻译前辈优越太多，切不可身在福中不知福。

对笔者而言，品文字、品翻译既是工作也是享受，这是第一重乐趣。更妙的是，在广泛涉猎中外报刊、品读中外经典的过程中，不断感受中外文化的碰撞与融通，并常常有所感有所悟。这是第二重乐趣。

林语堂从中西建筑风格差异看到中西方人生观、世界观和宗教观的差异："中国式屋顶不似哥特式尖塔那般直插云霄（天国）。……中国人最大的成就是在尘世中求得和谐与快乐（attain a measure of harmony and happiness in this earthly life）。"（《吾国与吾民》）

什么是"在尘世中求得和谐与快乐"？笔者最喜欢的中国文人苏轼就是典范。苏轼的一生感受过辉煌与黯淡、燃烧与宁静、欢乐与痛苦，其文学才华本足以照耀千古，但苏轼真正令后世钦仰的，是他面对命运与苦难时彰显的人格魅力。林语堂著英文版《苏东坡传》，书名是 *The Gay Genius*。"Gay"是形容词"快乐的、愉快的"，翻译过来就是"快乐的天才"。苏轼之所以成为中国人的精神榜样，正是因为他能在尘世的苦难中求得和谐与快乐。用佛家的话说，就是在尘世中求得"大自在"。

一个人顺风顺水时得出的人生观往往是虚妄的，只有历经磨难之后对人生的体悟才是最真实的。奥地利精神病学家维克多·弗兰克（犹太人大屠杀幸存者）在历尽命运的折磨后这样谈人生意义：

> 如果人生有意义，那么人生的苦难也必然有意义。苦难是人生不可或缺的一部分，正如命运与死亡也是。没有苦难与死亡，人生便不能圆满。……一个人接受命运与苦难的方式可以赋予他生命更深刻的意义。（*Man's Search for Meaning*）

品中外经典，阅古今中外精彩人生，丰富对人生的理解，企及恍然而悟的大自在，这是国际传播工作者的精神享受。

英国作家毛姆把阅读比作"躲避人生大部分苦难（饥饿之苦与单相思之苦除外）的庇护所"。写作本书，是一场愉快的旅行，在阅读和思考中躲避现实的烦恼，感受充实之乐。收笔那一刻，甚至有一丝不舍。泰戈尔告诉我们，体悟到"充实圆满"的那一刻，实在是比拥有的"果实"更加珍贵。

When we rejoice in our fullness, then we can part with our fruits with joy.

当我们以充实为乐时，便能快乐地跟我们的果实分手了。(《飞鸟集》)

希望这颗"果实"能给读者带去充实与快乐。

图书在版编目（CIP）数据

译路行远：跨越差异的国际传播 / 刘强著 . -- 北京：外文出版社，2024.3
（"译中国"文库）
ISBN 978-7-119-13817-6

Ⅰ . ①译… Ⅱ . ①刘… Ⅲ . ①传播学 – 文集②翻译 – 文集 Ⅳ . ① G206-53 ② H059-53

中国国家版本馆 CIP 数据核字 (2023) 第 237952 号

出版指导：胡开敏
出版统筹：许　荣
项目统筹：文　芳
项目协调：熊冰頔
英文审校：刘奎娟
责任编辑：张丽娟
装帧设计：星火设计实验室
印刷监制：章云天

译路行远
跨越差异的国际传播

刘　强　著

© 2024 外文出版社有限责任公司
出 版 人：胡开敏
出版发行：外文出版社有限责任公司
地　　址：中国北京西城区百万庄大街 24 号 邮政编码：100037
网　　址：http://www.flp.com.cn 电子邮箱：flp@cipg.org.cn
电　　话：008610-68320579（总编室）
　　　　　008610-68995861（编辑部）
　　　　　008610-68995852（发行部）
印　　刷：北京盛通印刷股份有限公司
开　　本：710mm×1000mm 1/16
字　　数：160 千字　　印　　张：13.75
装　　别：平装
版　　次：2024 年 3 月第 1 版第 1 次印刷
书　　号：ISBN 978-7-119-13817-6
定　　价：48.00 元

版权所有 侵权必究 如有印装问题本社负责调换（电话：010-68329904）